THE HARLEM
RENAISSANCE IN
AMERICAN HISTORY

The IN AMERICAN HISTORY Series

The African-American Struggle
for Legal Equality
(ISBN 0-7660-1415-0)

The Alaska Purchase
(ISBN 0-7660-1138-0)

Alcatraz Prison
(ISBN 0-89490-990-8)

The Battle of Gettysburg
(ISBN 0-7660-1455-X)

The Bombing of Pearl Harbor
(ISBN 0-7660-1126-7)

The Boston Tea Party
(ISBN 0-7660-1139-9)

The California Gold Rush
(ISBN 0-89490-878-2)

Charles Lindbergh and the
Spirit of St. Louis
(ISBN 0-7660-1683-8)

The Chisholm Trail
(ISBN 0-7660-1345-6)

The Confederacy and the Civil War
(ISBN 0-7660-1417-7)

The Cuban Missile Crisis
(ISBN 0-7660-1414-2)

The Dust Bowl and the Depression
(ISBN 0-7660-1838-5)

The Fight for Women's Right to Vote
(ISBN 0-89490-986-X)

The Great Depression
(ISBN 0-89490-881-2)

The Industrial Revolution
(ISBN 0-89490-985-1)

Jamestown, John Smith, and Pocahontas
(ISBN 0-7660-1842-3)

Japanese-American Internment
(ISBN 0-89490-767-0)

The Jim Crow Laws and Racism
(ISBN 0-7660-1297-2)

John Brown's Raid on Harpers Ferry
(ISBN 0-7660-1123-2)

Lewis and Clark's Journey of Discovery
(ISBN 0-7660-1127-5)

The Lincoln Assassination
(ISBN 0-89490-886-3)

The Lindbergh Baby Kidnapping
(ISBN 0-7660-1299-9)

The Little Rock School
Desegregation Crisis
(ISBN 0-7660-1298-0)

The Louisiana Purchase
(ISBN 0-7660-1301-4)

The Manhattan Project
and the Atomic Bomb
(ISBN 0-89490-879-0)

McCarthy and the Fear of Communism
(ISBN 0-89490-987-8)

The Mission Trails
(ISBN 0-7660-1349-9)

The Mormon Trail
and the Latter-day Saints
(ISBN 0-89490-988-6)

The Natchez Trace Historic Trail
(ISBN 0-7660-1344-8)

Nat Turner's Slave Rebellion
(ISBN 0-7660-1302-2)

The Oregon Trail
(ISBN 0-89490-771-9)

The Panama Canal
(ISBN 0-7660-1216-6)

The Pony Express
(ISBN 0-7660-1296-4)

The Pullman Strike and
the Labor Movement
(ISBN 0-7660-1300-6)

Reconstruction Following the Civil War
(ISBN 0-7660-1140-2)

The Salem Witchcraft Trials
(ISBN 0-7660-1125-9)

The Santa Fe Trail
(ISBN 0-7660-1348-0)

Shays' Rebellion and the Constitution
(ISBN 0-7660-1418-5)

Slavery and Abolition
(ISBN 0-7660-1124-0)

The Space Shuttle *Challenger* Disaster
(ISBN 0-7660-1419-3)

The Transcontinental Railroad
(ISBN 0-89490-882-0)

The Underground Railroad
(ISBN 0-89490-885-5)

The Union and the Civil War
(ISBN 0-7660-1416-9)

The Vietnam Antiwar Movement
(ISBN 0-7660-1295-6)

The Watergate Scandal
(ISBN 0-89490-883-9)

Westward Expansion and
Manifest Destiny
(ISBN 0-7660-1457-6)

IN
AMERICAN
HISTORY

THE HARLEM RENAISSANCE IN AMERICAN HISTORY

Ann Graham Gaines

Enslow Publishers, Inc.

40 Industrial Road   PO Box 38
Box 398   Aldershot
Berkeley Heights, NJ 07922   Hants GU12 6BP
USA   UK

http://www.enslow.com

Library of Congress Cataloging-in-Publication Data

Gaines, Ann.
    The Harlem Renaissance in American history / Ann Graham Gaines.
    Includes bibliographical references (p.   ) and index.
    ISBN 0-7660-1458-4
    1. African Americans—Intellectual life—20th century—Juvenile
literature. 2. Harlem Renaissance—Juvenile literature. 3. African American
arts—History—20th century—Juvenile literature. 4. Harlem (New York,
N.Y.)—Intellectual life—20th century—Juvenile literature. 5. African
Americans—New York (State)—New York—Intellectual life—20th
century—Juvenile literature. 6. African American arts—New York
(State)—New York–History—20th century—Juvenile literature. 7. New
York (N.Y.)—Intellectual life—20th century—Juvenile literature.
    [1. Harlem Renaissance. 2. African Americans—History—1877–1964.
3. African American arts. 4. Harlem (New York, N.Y.)—History.] I. Title.
II. Series.
    E185.6 .G135   2002
    974.7′100496073—dc21
                                                            2001001697

Printed in the United States of America

10 9 8 7 6 5 4 3 2 1

To Our Readers: We have done our best to make sure all Internet addresses in
this book were active and appropriate when we went to press. However, the
author and the publisher have no control over and assume no liability for the
material available on those Internet sites or on other Web sites they may link to.
Any comments or suggestions can be sent by e-mail to comments@enslow.com or
to the address on the back cover.

★ CONTENTS ★

1 Rent Parties 7

2 African Americans
    After the Civil War 13

3 Harlem, New York, and
    the Great Migration 31

4 The Renaissance Begins 40

5 Music and the Theater 63

6 Art 77

7 The End of the
    Harlem Renaissance 86

8 The Legacy of the
    Harlem Renaissance 94

    Timeline 100

    Chapter Notes 103

    Further Reading and
    Internet Addresses 110

    Index 111

RENT PARTIES

Harlem was a very exciting place to live during the 1920s. In fact, to African Americans, this neighborhood in New York City seemed like the most desirable place on Earth to live. Black people from all over the United States and the islands of the Caribbean dreamed of moving to Harlem because of its large African-American population, its many job opportunities, and its exciting nightlife.

But Harlem was expensive as well as exciting. In the 1920s, rents soared sky high, even for tiny apartments or a room in a house. Harlem was home to many African-American professionals—including doctors, lawyers, and ministers. High rents did not pose a problem for them. But most Harlem residents worked for small salaries. There were many jobs, but not all paid well. Many women from Harlem worked as laundresses or maids. Many men were porters, bellboys, bootblacks, or truck drivers.

Aspiring writers, artists, musicians, dancers, and actors had also moved to Harlem in great numbers. Many achieved success, selling poems or paintings or getting hired by a band or theater. Even

A fashionable African-American woman sits on a piano bench in Harlem.

so, they ran out of money on occasion.

To solve the problem of how to pay the rent, an enterprising resident of Harlem invented the rent party. By definition, a rent party was a party to which guests paid admission. The host used the money collected to pay rent. The idea of the rent party may have come from "parlor socials," which many African-American church groups held to raise money. Members made a small donation and were admitted to the social, which featured refreshments and music.[1] By the late 1920s, one Harlem resident remembered going to a rent party almost every single Saturday night.[2]

Short of cash, a writer might decide he needed to have a rent party. He would scrape together enough money to pay a printer for dozens of invitations on bright paper. He then plastered the neighborhood with them, tacking or taping them on electric poles and shop windows. Writer Frank Byrd's rent party invitation read:

If your life is bound
by convention and your
conduct always
above
reproach / tear this paper into
as many pieces as
possible
but—
If you dare to be
Entirely Emancipated
for one evening, then
come to
frank byrd's party . . .[3]

People with less education put up this invitation:

. . . if you ain't got nothin to do
Come on up to roy and sadie's
West 126 St. Sat. Night, May 12th . . .
Jus ring the bell an come on in. . . .[4]

On the night of a rent party, people poured through the door. Some were the host's friends and neighbors. Many guests were strangers. Every guest put a little money—perhaps a few dimes or a quarter—into a hat or a jar when they arrived. It seemed a small price to pay, since it entitled one to enjoy plenty of food, drink, and live music.

Liquor was outlawed all across the United States during the 1920s because of Prohibition. It was illegal to buy, sell, or drink alcoholic beverages. Nevertheless, people who went to rent parties sometimes found bottles of beer sitting in buckets of ice. Expensive imported liquor from Scotland or homemade grain alcohol might be available, too. Some Harlem residents drove out into the country to buy illegal liquor. Others made it themselves in bathtubs.

Soon the sound of lively and danceable music drifted out onto the street from an open window. The party's host would have invited musicians to play in exchange for part of the money he raised. The musicians might bring drums, saxophones, or trumpets. Piano players performed. Often the jazz players simply improvised very late at night, making up the music as they went along. That was something they loved but were not allowed to do in the neighborhood's fancy nightclubs. Everybody danced. Rent parties often lasted all night long.

Rent parties were more than fun. Sometimes, they also served as inspiration to a writer or songwriter. Days, weeks, months, even years later, a writer might make his rent party the subject of a poem or describe it in a novel.[5] Years later, writers who had lived in Harlem during the 1920s described in glowing detail rent parties in their memoirs.[6] Jazz great Fats Waller wrote a hit song, "The Joint Is Jumpin'" about a rent party. It included the lines:

> *Be sure to pay your quarter*
> *Burn your leather on the floor*
> *Grab [dance with] anybody's daughter*
> *The roof is rockin'*
> *The neighbor's knockin'*

We're all bums when the wagon comes
I said the joint is jumpin'.[7]

Rent parties were a hallmark of the Harlem Renaissance. Few people used the phrase Harlem Renaissance back then, but today historians use it to describe the African-American cultural movement that took place between about 1919 and 1929. The movement was centered in Harlem but it spread elsewhere, too. For centuries, Africans had been limited in terms of opportunities they were offered in Europe and the United States. African Americans had a long, proud musical tradition, but the songs they sang in the fields or at church seldom became popular with the white majority where they lived. However, during the Harlem Renaissance, there was a "dramatic upsurge of creativity in literature, music, and art within black America," as historian Arnold Rampersad explained.[8] In Harlem especially, African-American writers produced poems, short stories, novels, plays, newspaper articles, and essays. They published dozens of books as well as hundreds of pieces in magazines. At the same time, musicians composed and performed both popular and classical music. African-American theater flourished. Artists created works in many different media—drawings, paintings, and sculpture.

During the Harlem Renaissance, the creative efforts of African Americans were also recognized and appreciated by the world in general. White audiences in the United States, Europe, the Caribbean, and other places began to pay attention to the cultural explosion that was going on in Harlem.

African-American writers, musicians, artists, and social and political activists met and mingled in Harlem. Whites who were interested in literature, art, and music became patrons of some blacks whom they regarded as creative geniuses. They gave financial support to writers and artists and helped get their works published and made known to the world outside of Harlem. As African-American artists began to receive both pay and appreciation for their creative works, more and more aspiring artists began to fill Harlem's bustling streets. There were more and more enthusiastic, creative people who interacted with each other. Together, they encouraged each other to pursue their creative inspirations. Soon, there was a movement—a Renaissance—in Harlem.

Creative minds inspired each other. Most of these people shared common goals. They worked to generate pride among African Americans, especially pride in their heritage. Harlem ranks as a place of great historical significance. Today, Harlem residents and other Americans express great pride in the creativity displayed during the Harlem Renaissance.

AFRICAN AMERICANS AFTER THE CIVIL WAR

When the Civil War ended in 1865, hundreds of thousands of African-American former slaves, now freed, were left with no skills. They were agricultural day laborers left in a land devastated by war. The vast majority of African Americans had worked for others their entire lives. Less than one percent of the newly freed African Americans owned the home they lived in, much less the land on which it stood.[1]

Many of these freed African Americans were worse off economically than they had been as slaves. Forced off the lands of their former owners, many newly freed African Americans moved to the nearest big city, owning absolutely nothing. More than ten thousand African Americans freed from the plantations of Louisiana moved to the city of New Orleans. Almost all these people had no money and no skills that employers desired. Labor agents from Northern states recruited African Americans to move to those states, but they were generally interested only in those who had skills. Many rural African-American families stayed close to their former homes and became sharecroppers. They used their

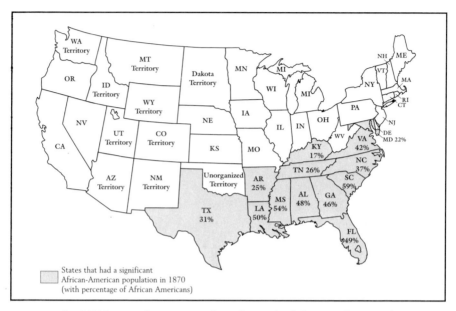

States that had a significant
African-American population in 1870
(with percentage of African Americans)

In 1870, just five years after the end of the Civil War, the vast majority of African Americans still lived in the Southern states.

landlord's land, tools, mules, and seed to farm a crop of cotton or corn. They paid the landlord for these loans when the crop was harvested and sold, often to the same landlord. Whatever was left in profit was then shared with the landlord. Often, the sharecropper worked an entire year for nothing but to be left burdened with a debt that would require him to do the same thing the next year.

Discrimination Continues

After the Civil War, local and state governments began passing many laws that segregated, or separated, the races in almost every possible public place. There were separate schools, restaurants, toilets, hotels, drinking fountains, and even cemeteries. In some Southern cities, laws stated which neighborhoods African Americans could live in.

To make matters worse, politicians also took away the right to vote from African Americans who had just recently won civil rights with the North's victory in the Civil War. African Americans were kept from voting in a number of ways. The state of Louisiana, for example, allowed only people whose ancestors had been registered to vote before the Civil War to vote in current elections. This, of course, automatically made the number of African-American voters very small indeed. Many towns also imposed a poll tax. This meant that only men with enough of an income to afford to pay a special voting tax could vote. Since most African Americans had no money whatsoever, poll taxes had the same effect as denying them the right to vote altogether.

But the lack of respect for their political rights was not the worst problem African Americans faced. Secret societies of whites tried to deny African Americans their rights. Organizations such as the Ku Klux Klan (KKK), lynched (murdered) African Americans who tried to vote and terrorized entire neighborhoods in an attempt to frighten African Americans out of trying to exercise their newly won rights.

Poor whites had to compete with the freed African Americans for employment. Wages paid for agricultural work on large farms, previously called plantations, were terrible. As late as 1880, a month's pay for work from sunrise to sunset was approximately ten dollars. Like blacks, many poor rural whites could not afford to pay poll taxes. They resented being put on the same level with the former slaves. All these conditions provoked conflict and hatred, especially in the South.

Some practical people saw that the slow solution—there was no quick fix—to ending racial tensions lay in teaching African Americans the skills that would help them either find decent jobs in the South or survive in the western frontier and Northern industrial cities. During these years, many African Americans were leaving the South in the hope of finding better job opportunities and, perhaps, less discrimination.

Booker T. Washington

Booker Taliaferro Washington was born in 1856, a slave child on a farm in the Virginia backcountry. After the Civil War, he moved with his family to West Virginia. There, he worked in salt factories and coal mines, doing back-breaking labor. When he heard about Hampton Institute, a secondary school founded for African Americans who worked in the coal mines, Washington became determined to attend. An education of any sort was a lofty goal in the minds of many of his neighbors. Many pitched in to help him make the trip. Washington later wrote,

> Perhaps the thing that touched and pleased me most in connection with my starting for Hampton was the interest that many of the older coloured people took in

Booker T. Washington's theories about economic self-sufficiency being necessary before equal rights made him a very controversial African-American leader.

the matter. They had spent the best days of their lives in slavery, and hardly expected to live to see the time when they would see a member of their race leave home to attend a boarding-school. Some of these older people would give me a nickel, others a quarter, or a handkerchief.[2]

The headmaster of the school, Samuel C. Chapman, was a Union veteran of the Civil War. He was greatly admired by his students for his upright and unselfish character. His ideals inspired his students, who felt that they were indeed creating the first wave of free African-American progress in the United States. According to Washington,

I was among the youngest of the students who were in Hampton at that time. Most of the students were men and women—some as old as forty years of age. As I now recall the scene of my first year, I do not believe that one often has the opportunity of coming into contact with three or four hundred men and women who were so tremendously in earnest as these men and women were. Every hour was occupied in study or work.[3]

After Washington graduated, he taught in Alabama before he borrowed the money to open his own school. The Tuskegee Institute was modeled after the educational philosophy of Samuel Chapman. It offered the basic academic high school courses but put an emphasis on teaching practical skills such as carpentry, shoemaking, printing, cabinetmaking, farming, and brick-making.

SOURCE DOCUMENT

FOR SOME MINUTES THERE WAS GREAT REJOICING, AND THANKSGIVING, AND WILD SCENES OF ECSTASY. BUT THERE WAS NO FEELING OF BITTERNESS. IN FACT, THERE WAS PITY AMONG THE SLAVES FOR OUR FORMER OWNERS. THE WILD REJOICING ON THE PART OF THE EMANCIPATED COLORED PEOPLE LASTED FOR BUT A BRIEF PERIOD, FOR I NOTICED THAT BY THE TIME THEY RETURNED TO THEIR CABINS THERE WAS A CHANGE IN THEIR FEELINGS. THE GREAT RESPONSIBILITY OF BEING FREE, OF HAVING CHARGE OF THEMSELVES, OF HAVING TO THINK AND PLAN FOR THEMSELVES AND THEIR CHILDREN, SEEMED TO TAKE POSSESSION OF THEM. IT WAS VERY MUCH LIKE SUDDENLY TURNING A YOUTH OF TEN OR TWELVE YEARS OUT INTO THE WORLD TO PROVIDE FOR HIMSELF.[4]

In his autobiography, Up From Slavery, *African-American leader Booker T. Washington described the reactions of his fellow former slaves when they learned that they were free.*

Washington made his school a success. He convinced both Northern and Southern bankers and politicians to support his work. It was not an easy thing to do. The attitude toward education for African Americans throughout the country was tainted with many racial prejudices and stereotypes. Many Southerners were afraid that education would give blacks not only economic power over poor whites, but also a desire to become politically powerful. Many whites felt that any education for blacks was too much.

The prevailing opinion among both Northern philanthropic foundations and Southern political leaders, however, was that the best secondary education for African Americans was to teach practical skills that would enable them to earn a good living and become a contributing part of the middle class of American workers. Many African-American leaders, especially later, criticized Booker T. Washington for an attitude that accepted white superiority in the higher levels of the society while holding out only the opportunity for lower goals for African Americans. He was criticized for his attitude of compliance with racist white ideas. Despite this hostility, many African Americans felt they benefited from his ideas, especially about education.

Many African Americans, who suffered under the oppression of sharecropping, constant debt, no medical treatment, and the fear of the KKK, found Washington's offer of self-employment, land ownership, employment skills, and a basic education highly desirable. Thousands attended the Tuskegee Institute, which, by 1900, was the best supported African-American school in the country. Booker T. Washington remained the foremost spokesman for African Americans until around 1905. He always preached accommodation, conciliation, patience, and the need to learn skills. He believed African Americans could only secure their rights if they first became economically independent and a respected part of American society.

African-American Literacy

Mostly on their own, African Americans began the fundamental education of their people. Under slavery, few African Americans were taught to read or write. In fact, in some places, it was a crime to teach a slave to read. By the 1880s, 30 percent of African Americans could read; by 1890, 50 percent could. By 1900, some African-American weekly newspapers had a national circulation of hundreds of thousands of readers. These newspapers employed African-American writers and editors. There were some African-American publishers devoted to putting out books for mostly African-American audiences. They published literature and history, as well as material for Sunday schools and church histories.[5] The number of African Americans whose books were published by main-stream publishers, however, was small.

By 1910, fully two thirds of the African-American population could read. Booker T. Washington and the unnamed thousands of African-American educators like him throughout the country had done their job well. They gave the vast majority of African Americans a foundation on which to erect a literary movement. The flowering of that movement would not take long once it had an audience to support it.

W.E.B. DuBois

William Edward Burghardt DuBois was born on February 23, 1868, in Great Barrington, Massachusetts. He was a gifted student and intellectual. In high school, he showed a deep concern for his fellow African Americans. At the age of fifteen, he became the local correspondent for the *New York Globe* newspaper and published articles that encouraged African Americans to become politically involved in government. He graduated from the local high school and received a scholarship to Fisk College in Nashville, Tennessee, in 1885. This was DuBois's first trip to the old South. There, he learned firsthand of the poverty, igno- rance, and prejudice

W.E.B. DuBois was one of the African-American leaders whose efforts in politics helped inspire the Harlem Renaissance.

that confronted African Americans. He graduated after three years at Fisk and went on to attend Harvard University in Cambridge, Massachusetts. After studying for a year at the University of Berlin in Germany, DuBois returned to Harvard to complete his doctoral dissertation, "The Suppression of the African Slave Trade in America." It remains the authoritative work on that subject and is the first volume in Harvard's Historical Series.

In 1896, after teaching for two years at Wilberforce College in Ohio, DuBois accepted a fellowship from the University of Pennsylvania to conduct a study of a local African-American neighborhood. He performed an exhaustive examination of the neighborhood and its problems. The study was published under the title *The Philadelphia Negro.* Next, DuBois accepted a position at Atlanta University to teach sociology. For the next thirteen years, DuBois studied and wrote on many different facets of African-American life, including morality, urbanization, businesses, religion, crime, and education.

Like Booker T. Washington, DuBois became convinced that education was the African American's first need. Unlike Washington, however, who wanted the greatest number of African Americans to achieve just the basic education that would lead to self-sufficiency, DuBois wanted a smaller percentage of African Americans who showed intellectual prominence, a group he called "the Talented Tenth," to go to college and become legislators and business

SOURCE DOCUMENT

... I HAVE HEARD THAT YOU ARE A YOUNG WOMAN OF SOME ABILITY BUT THAT YOU ARE NEGLECTING YOUR SCHOOL WORK BECAUSE YOU HAVE BECOME HOPELESS OF TRYING TO DO ANYTHING IN THE WORLD. I AM VERY SORRY FOR THIS. HOW ANY HUMAN BEING WHOSE WONDERFUL FORTUNE IT IS TO LIVE IN THE 20TH CENTURY SHOULD UNDER ORDINARILY FAIR ADVANTAGES DESPAIR OF LIFE IS ALMOST UNBELIEVABLE. AND IF IN ADDITION TO THIS THAT PERSON IS, AS I AM, OF NEGRO LINEAGE WITH ALL THE HOPES AND YEARNINGS OF HUNDREDS OF MILLIONS OF HUMAN SOULS DEPENDENT IN SOME DEGREE ON HER STRIVING, THEN HER BITTERNESS AMOUNTS TO A CRIME.

THERE ARE IN THE U.S. TODAY TENS OF THOUSANDS OF COLORED GIRLS WHO WOULD BE HAPPY BEYOND MEASURE TO HAVE THE CHANCE OF EDUCATING THEMSELVES THAT YOU ARE NEGLECTING.[6]

W.E.B. DuBois wrote this letter to a young girl named Vernealia Fareira, urging her to take her education more seriously and to have hope for the future.

leaders. From these positions of power, DuBois said, the Talented Tenth could pass laws and create jobs that would more quickly bring African Americans the economic and legal standards that were the first step to real racial equality.

DuBois published a book called *The Souls of Black Folks.*[7] In this work, DuBois showed the fine literary style and inspirational fire that made his works compelling to readers of any race:

The history of the American Negro is the history of this strife,—this longing to attain self-conscious manhood, to merge his double self into a better and truer self. In this merging he wishes neither of the older selves to be lost. He would not Africanize America, for America has too much to teach the world and Africa. He would not bleach the Negro soul in a flood of white Americanism, for he knows that Negro blood has a message for the world. He simply wishes to make it possible for a man to be both a Negro and an American, without being cursed and spit upon by his fellows, without having the doors of Opportunity closed roughly in his face.[8]

Published by a white publishing firm, *The Souls of Black Folks* sold very well. It got little attention in white Southern newspapers, however. *The New York Times* gave it scant praise. The paper concluded that what DuBois really wanted was to "smoke a cigar and drink a cup of tea with the white man in the South."[9] But the *Nation* and the *New York Evening Post* praised DuBois's work as a well-written and challenging book.[10] It sold ten thousand copies in five years, a remarkable figure for a controversial book.[11]

The Niagara Movement

In 1905, DuBois became convinced that he and other African Americans had to make a more aggressive move to achieve racial equality. It was not enough simply to write about it. He became an activist.

In January 1906, DuBois and twenty-nine other men from fourteen states met across the Canadian border from Buffalo, New York. There, they formed a society whose objectives were to bring about civil justice, abolish discrimination, and win universal suffrage for all American males, regardless of race or class. They called their organization the Niagara Movement. Members of the Niagara Movement publicized their cause, giving speeches and writing about their goals.

The group never raised much money and it also suffered from accusations of fraud and deceit. These charges were brought forth by dissatisfied Booker T. Washington supporters, who viewed the group as too radical for the good of African Americans.

In 1909, all of the members of the Niagara Movement except one joined with white activists and formed the National Association for the Advancement of Colored People (NAACP).[12] W.E.B. DuBois became the director of publications and research for the organization and the editor of its magazine, *The Crisis*. DuBois remained the fiery editor for twenty-five years. In an excerpt from the March 1913 issue, entitled "The Proper Way," DuBois wrote:

> What is possible to-day and to-morrow and every day is to keep up necessary agitation, make unfaltering protest, fill the courts and legislatures and executive chambers, and keep everlastingly at the work of protest in season and out of season. The weak and silly part of the program of those who deprecate complaint and agitation is that a moment's let up, a moment's acquiescence, means a chance for the wolves of prejudice to get at our necks. It is not that we have too many organizations; it is that we have too few effective workers in the great cause of Negro emancipation in America. Let us from this movement

join in a frontal attack on disfranchisement, "Jim Crow" cars and lynching. We shall not win to-day or to-morrow, but some day we shall win if we faint not.[13]

African-American Writers at the Turn of the Century

While W.E.B. DuBois was becoming the spokesman for the political movement that worked to bring racial equality to the United States, there were other African Americans who began to work outside the movement. These people hoped to give the white audience a picture of the evils of slavery and prejudice derived from the African-American experience. These early poets and novelists were often neglected by the mainstream culture of America. The vast majority of the book-buying public in America in 1900 was white. Whites were seldom ready to pay money to be told about their racial prejudices and social obligations. In many cases, African-American writers of first-rate quality could find no one to publish their works. However, a few African-American writers did achieve a general audience during this time.

Charles Waddell Chestnutt

Charles Waddell Chestnutt was born in North Carolina in 1858. For several years, Chestnutt taught at what is now Fayetteville State University in North Carolina before he moved to Cleveland, Ohio, and passed the bar examination to become a lawyer. He opened a successful stenographic business and turned his attention to his first love, writing. When he was twenty-nine years old, he became the first African American to have a work published in a major American magazine, *Atlantic Monthly.*

Chestnutt continued to write essays, folktales, short stories, and novels. In his eight published novels, Chestnutt addressed many problems and gave his mainly white audience a new view of the black man. His best-known book, *The Conjure Woman,* published in 1899, is a collection of African-American slave tales from the Cape Fear region of North Carolina he remembered from his boyhood. *The House Behind the Cedars* was published in 1900. It was a tale set in North Carolina that dealt with the problems of children of racially mixed couples. *The Marrow of Tradition* was set during the Wilmington, North Carolina, race riot of 1898. Chestnutt was a regular contributor to some of the most prestigious and successful magazines of the times: *Atlantic Monthly, Century Magazine, The Outlook, Self Culture*, and *Southern Workman.*[14]

Paul Laurence Dunbar

Paul Laurence Dunbar, the son of former slaves, was the only African-American student in Central High School in Dayton, Ohio, in 1890. There, he wrote and edited a four-page weekly called *The Tattler.* His printer and schoolmate was Orville Wright, who later went on to become, with his brother Wilbur, the inventor of the airplane. The two young men were good friends. Dunbar wrote a poem on the wall of Wright's print shop:

> *Orville Wright is out of sight*
> *In the printing business.*
> *No other mind is half so bright*
> *As his'n is.*[15]

Dunbar continued to write and approached Orville Wright to print a book of his collected poems. Wright's print shop could print but not bind the books, so Dunbar approached Wright's father's print shop, the United Brethren publishers in Dayton. Dunbar used $125 of the money he earned from his four-dollar-a-week job as an elevator operator in town to print five hundred copies of *Oak and Ivy*. The book won him acclaim as a poet and scholar around the country.[16] His second book, *Majors and Minors*, revealed Dunbar's fine poetic style, as shown in an excerpt from his poem, "The Colored Soldiers":

> *In the early days you scorned them,*
> *And with many a flip and flout,*
> *Said "these battles are the white man's*
> *And the whites will fight them out."*
> *Up the hills you fought and faltered,*
> *In the vales you strove and bled,*
> *While your ears still heard the thunder*
> *Of the foes' increasing tread.*
> *Then distress fell on the nation*
> *And the flag was drooping low;*
> *Should the dust pollute your banner?*
> *No! the nation shouted, No!*

Paul Laurence Dunbar, who was a childhood friend of the Wright brothers, became famous for his poetry.

So when war, in savage triumph,
Spread abroad his funeral pall—
Then you called the colored soldiers,
And they answered to your call.

And like hounds unleashed and eager
For the life blood of the prey,
Sprung they forth and bore them bravely
In the thickest of the fray.
And where'er the fight was hottest—
Where the bullets fastest fell,
There they pressed unblanched and fearless.
At the very mouth of hell.[17]

Later, Dunbar also published four novels. The last of these, *Sport of the Gods*, was published in 1902. The novel tells the story of the Hamiltons, a middle-class African-American family living in the South, who are destroyed by the hatred of their white employers, the Oakleys. Berry Hamilton, the father, is convicted of a crime he did not commit and his family is forced to move to Harlem. At the time, Harlem was just beginning to be a place to which a large number of African Americans from the South were moving. Dunbar's novel served as a warning that racial prejudice and the evils of big-city life were as real in New York as they were in the rural South. Joe Hamilton, the teenage son of the family, becomes an alcoholic and eventually commits murder. The mother and daughter leave Harlem and return to the South.

One of the novel's messages is that racial hatred in both the North and the South continued to destroy the lives of African Americans. *Sport of the Gods* was not especially popular at the time of its publication. Few whites were prepared to acknowledge the effects of their racial prejudices. Four years later, Dunbar died of tuberculosis in 1906. He was only thirty-three years old.

3

HARLEM, NEW YORK, AND THE GREAT MIGRATION

When Paul Laurence Dunbar's novel *Sport of the Gods* was published in 1902, nearly 90 percent of African Americans lived in the states of the old South. Almost 80 percent of these still lived in rural settings. Shortly after 1900 and continuing through the 1920s, large numbers of African Americans began to move to the large industrial cities of the Midwest and Northeast. It is estimated that between 700,000 and one million African Americans left the states of the South between 1917 and 1920. Another million left during the 1920s. In the Midwest, the African-American population of Detroit increased more than 600 percent during World War I (1914–1918) and increased from 6,000 in 1900 to over 120,000 by the end of the 1920s. New York City and Philadelphia, Pennsylvania, in the Northeast and Chicago, Illinois, in the Midwest saw the most dramatic increases in their African-American populations. Between 1910 and 1930, Chicago's African-American population rose from 44,000 to over 234,000,

Philadelphia's from 84,000 to 220,000; and New York's, most of whom lived in just the large neighborhood of Harlem on Manhattan, increased from 100,000 to over 325,000. This fundamental shift in the African-American population of the United States is known as the Great Migration.

Causes of the Great Migration

Most of the African Americans who left the South in such great numbers during this time were extremely glad to escape what had been a hard life. Racism existed on a large scale in the South. African Americans were allowed few good job opportunities. Most lived in miserable houses in isolated sections of the country.

Adding to the generally poor living conditions endured by African Americans in the South, was an attitude among them that things were not going to get any better. It had been forty years since the end of the Civil War and conditions were not improving for most African Americans. Economic conditions were still terrible for the small farmer, and even worse for the unskilled laborer. Racial prejudice had become a way of life.

Conditions were much better in the North. The vast waves of European immigration to the United States had brought more than 14 million people from Europe between 1870 and 1900 and another 9 million between 1900 and 1910. By the time of the Great Migration, however, immigration was beginning to be slowed by restrictive laws that tried to prevent

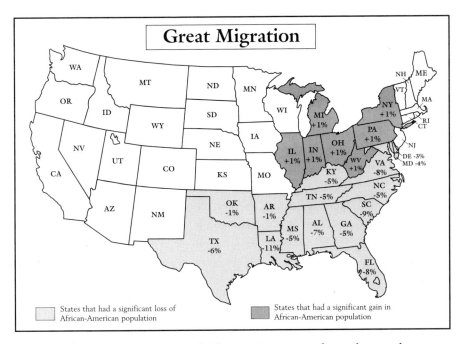

Great Migration

States that had a significant loss of African-American population

States that had a significant gain in African-American population

The Great Migration of African Americans from the rural South to the industrial North dramatically changed the makeup of Northern cities' populations.

foreign-born people from taking jobs away from native-born Americans. World War I, which began in 1914, further slowed European immigration. In 1914, more than a million European immigrants came to the United States. By 1916, there were hardly 250,000 European immigrants, and by 1918, there were only 110,000—almost exactly the number of Europeans who returned to their native lands.

All of a sudden, the large labor market in the North that had been satisfied earlier by foreign immigrants needed new workers to continue to grow. By 1915, Northern industries had set up recruiting stations throughout the South to convince African-American

Macon Ga April 21/18

To the Bethenlem Baptist Associa
tion reading in the chicaga
Defender of your help
securing positions I want
to Know if it is any way
you can oblige me by
helping me to get out
there as I am anxious
to leave here + every
thing so hard here I hope
you will oblige in help
ing me to leave here
ans at once to 304
middle St. Mrs J. H. Adam

African Americans were eager to explore the job
opportunities available to them in the North, as the
writer of this letter from Macon, Georgia, expresses.

workers to move to the North. Railroads also sent recruiters to publicize the better jobs available for African Americans in the North. Many Southern African Americans saw this as a great opportunity. They eagerly moved north to take steady and better-paid industrial jobs.[1]

Harlem

The Great Migration brought thousands of African Americans to Harlem, the largest African-American neighborhood in New York City. Like many neighborhoods in New York, its boundaries have changed over time. In 1920, it was a large neighborhood of handsome brick buildings, wide streets, and little pollution. In 1930, Harlem stretched from Park Avenue in the east to Eighth Avenue in the west. The Harlem River and 159th Street formed its northern boundary. On the south, the boundary was roughly 126th Street, although it dipped down to include the big pocket of African Americans who lived in the area between Eighth and Fifth avenues, just north of Central Park.[2]

American Indians had long fished and farmed in the area when Dutch colonists began to settle the northern part of Manhattan Island in 1658. The Dutch called the neighborhood of small farms Nieuw Harlem. In 1664, British colonists forced the Dutch out of the area. British officials wanted to rename the place Lancaster. But local residents continued to refer to it by its old name, changing its spelling to "Harlem."

A view of Seventh Avenue in Harlem, New York City, during the Harlem Renaissance.

By the eighteenth century, Harlem became the site of some important historic events. During the American Revolution, the Battle of Harlem Heights was fought there. On September 15, 1776, British troops captured downtown New York and pushed American General George Washington's troops to the north, into Harlem Heights. The Americans held off the British advance in a six-hour battle. It was the only

American victory of the early British campaign against New York.

After the war, Harlem Heights became a small town populated mainly by Irish immigrants. Harlem remained a rural community until the late nineteenth century. By 1873, New York City had grown enough to annex Harlem.[3] In fact, New York City was growing in all directions.

African Americans Move to Harlem

In the early twentieth century, the Lenox Avenue subway opened for business. It gave working people the chance to live in Harlem and commute to their jobs downtown. At this time, the population of Harlem was largely English and German, with increasing numbers of Jewish immigrants from Eastern Europe.

In 1904, Philip A. Payton, Jr., an African-American realtor, founded the Afro-American Realty Company. His plan was to rent vacant buildings in the neighborhood and sublease their apartments to other African Americans. He first put tenants into houses on 134th Street. Payton's company existed for only four years, but it was instrumental in bringing a number of African Americans to the neighborhood. His realty also helped establish Harlem's reputation as an African-American neighborhood.

In earlier years, the largest number of African Americans in Manhattan lived in areas known as the Tenderloin and San Juan Hill. These were rough neighborhoods, densely populated slums that saw a lot of crime.[4] In the early 1900s, middle-class African-American residents of New York wanted better housing. They realized that Harlem would be a nice place to live. So when realtors began to rent apartments to African Americans, many took advantage of the opportunity and moved to the uptown neighborhood.[5] At the same time, African-American migrants arrived from the South and came to live in Harlem. Other new residents came from the Caribbean Islands and Latin America. As the African-American population of Harlem increased, African-American churches and businesses moved there. So did professionals such as doctors, dentists, and lawyers.[6] Harlem became an African-American community.[7]

Mecca

To African Americans, Harlem seemed like a mecca, or center of activity. James Weldon Johnson, the editor of an influential African-American magazine, wrote about Harlem in 1925: "Throughout colored America, from Massachusetts to Mississippi, and across the continent to Los Angeles and Seattle, its name, which as late as fifteen years ago had scarcely been heard, now stands for the Negro metropolis."[8]

Residents liked the place and felt proud to live there. African Americans who lived elsewhere in the United States often wanted to move to Harlem. They kept track of what went on there. To both whites and blacks, Harlem became a place of excitement and hope.[9]

One of the greatest attractions for African Americans was just how many blacks lived in Harlem. James Weldon Johnson noted that a stranger who crossed 125th Street "rides through twenty-five solid blocks where the passers-by, the shoppers, those sitting in restaurants, coming out of theaters, standing in doorways and looking out of windows are practically all Negroes."[10] It was an entire community. It held not just places to live, but also businesses, churches, social and civic centers, and many sources of entertainment. It was home to the headquarters of both the NAACP and the Urban League, two leading national African-American organizations.

In 1920, 150,000 African Americans lived in Harlem.[11] A new, literate African-American population had completely taken over a sizable section of the largest, most vibrant city in the United States. Now the many talents of people from all parts of the United States and the Caribbean islands came together to create a flowering of African-American culture.

4

THE RENAISSANCE BEGINS

On February 19, 1919, crowds lined the streets of New York City. They had gathered to watch the African-American 369th U.S. Army Regiment march to Harlem.[1] The regiment was just home from fighting in World War I. It was an occasion when African Americans felt great pride.

During the 1920s, members of the African-American community of Harlem felt confidence in themselves and their abilities. As a result, they showed enormous creativity. This joyous creativity was expressed through all types of art, music, and literature.

Over the next ten years, this pride would grow. African-American artists and intellectuals in Harlem would set out to help not only the their own community but the entire United States to recognize African-American accomplishments.

This growing pride in being African-American was a reflection of the general attitude of the whole Harlem neighborhood. It was the attitude of "the street"— it could be seen in barber shops, bars, restaurants, and clubs of Harlem. People were happy to be

Harlem was filled with bustling activity. This view of the corner of Seventh Avenue and West 138th Street shows some of the thriving businesses of the area.

African-American, to express themselves in unique ways of dressing, dancing, singing, writing, and painting. One of the men who seized upon this wellspring of African-American pride was politician and human-rights leader Marcus Garvey.

Marcus Garvey

Marcus Garvey was a great force for social and political change during the 1920s. He was one of the most influential African-American political leaders of the twentieth century. Today, reformers still draw on his example for inspiration.

Marcus Garvey was born in Jamaica in 1887. As a young man, he worked as a printer. In 1910, when he had saved enough money, he left his homeland to travel first to Central America and then to England. There, his interest in politics began. He became a Pan-Africanist—a believer in the need for people of African descent, no matter where they lived, to unite to fight for their rights.

In 1914, he went home to Jamaica and founded the Universal Negro Improvement Association (UNIA).

SOURCE DOCUMENT

BEING BLACK, I HAVE COMMITTED AN UNPARDONABLE OFFENSE AGAINST THE VERY LIGHT COLORED NEGROES IN AMERICA AND THE WEST INDIES BY MAKING MYSELF FAMOUS AS A NEGRO LEADER OF MILLIONS. IN THEIR VIEW, NO BLACK MAN MUST RISE ABOVE THEM, BUT I STILL FORGE AHEAD DETERMINED TO GIVE TO THE WORLD THE TRUTH ABOUT THE NEW NEGRO WHO IS DETERMINED TO MAKE AND HOLD FOR HIMSELF A PLACE IN THE AFFAIRS OF MEN. THE UNIVERSAL NEGRO IMPROVEMENT ASSOCIATION HAS BEEN MISREPRESENTED BY MY ENEMIES. THEY HAVE TRIED TO MAKE IT APPEAR THAT WE ARE HOSTILE TO OTHER RACES. THIS IS ABSOLUTELY FALSE. WE LOVE ALL HUMANITY. WE ARE WORKING FOR THE PEACE OF THE WORLD WHICH WE BELIEVE CAN ONLY COME ABOUT WHEN ALL RACES ARE GIVEN THEIR DUE.[2]

Marcus Garvey, the controversial leader of UNIA, wrote this statement about his organization's goals.

Marcus Garvey's UNIA held parades to promote its cause.

He wanted to pass on his ideas concerning Pan-Africanism, as well as encourage other African Americans to help themselves. He preached the need for African Americans to learn skills and help themselves to succeed. He believed African Americans should build their own economy, supporting each other.

In March 1916, he emigrated to the United States, settling in Harlem. There he reestablished the UNIA and started an enormously popular self-help movement. He believed in the need for racial pride and emphasized African Americans' need to know their own history.

Garvey started a "Back to Africa" movement. The UNIA planned to raise money to buy a ship and take

African Americans to Africa to live. The members of the UNIA wore uniforms and staged parades to help popularize their ideas. Garvey supported self-rule for all of Africa. He promised Africans that he would help them overthrow the colonial governments that ruled their lands.

James Weldon Johnson

Marcus Garvey intentionally appealed to people of African descent only. Other black leaders and artists, on the other hand, tried to win white support to help foster black pride.

James Weldon Johnson was born in Jacksonville, Florida, on June 17, 1871. His mother, Helen, was the first African-American woman to teach in a public school in Florida. After graduating from Atlanta University in 1894, Johnson returned to Jacksonville and became principal of the Stanton School, the eight-year school he had attended as a boy. He converted it to a twelve-year school.

Johnson studied to become a lawyer. He was one of the first African Americans to be admitted to the Florida Bar in 1897. He also became the owner, publisher, and editor of the *Daily American*, an African-American daily newspaper in Duval County. In his spare time, he wrote an opera with his brother.[3] Johnson was a man who seized life and made of it what he willed. He did not let the bigotry and prejudice of the Reconstruction South stand in his way. He wrote,

I will not allow one prejudiced person or one million or one hundred million to blight my life. I will not let prejudice or any of its attendant humiliations and injustices bear me down to spiritual defeat. My inner life is mine, and I shall defend and maintain its integrity against all the powers of hell.[4]

In 1899, in collaboration with his brother, Johnson published the lyrics to the song that soon became the African-American national anthem, "Lift Every Voice and Sing":

Lift every voice and sing
Till earth and heaven ring,
Ring with the harmonies of Liberty;
Let our rejoicing rise
High as the listening skies,
Let it resound loud as the rolling sea.
Sing a song full of the faith that the dark past has taught us,
Sing a song full of the hope that the present has brought us,
Facing the rising sun of our new day begun
Let us march on till victory is won. . . .[5]

Also in 1899, Johnson and his brother went to New York to get their opera produced. They failed in this, but they returned to the city the next year and formed a partnership with Bob Cole, a noted African-American composer of popular songs. For the next seven years, the trio wrote many of the most popular tunes of the day. They traveled to Europe and were booked at the Palace Theater for a week in 1905.

Johnson returned to New York to study literature at Columbia University. He became a Republican and wrote a tune called "You're All Right, Teddy," for the presidential campaign of Theodore Roosevelt. After Roosevelt won the election, Johnson was appointed to the consular service of the United States in Venezuela in 1906.[6] Johnson married Grace Nail and the couple moved to Nicaragua, where he continued in the consular service.

In 1912, Johnson's book *The Autobiography of an Ex-Colored Man* was published. It received little attention at first, but was reprinted in 1925 during the Harlem Renaissance. It was then recognized as an important book.

Johnson returned to New York and became the field secretary of the NAACP in 1916. During 1920 and 1921, he led the NAACP's campaign to pass a federal antilynching bill. His intense lobbying helped the bill pass in the House of Representatives. When the bill failed to pass the Senate, Johnson was a member of the African-American delegation that appealed personally to President Warren Harding for support.

He continued to work for the NAACP during the 1920s. Eventually, he became the organization's executive secretary. Johnson quickly became one of the most influential African-American leaders in America. Carl Van Vechten, an influential white editor, described him: "So warm was his humanity, so complete his tact, and so amazing his social skill that he was the master of any situation in which he found himself."[7]

SOURCE DOCUMENT

AND GOD STEPPED OUT ON SPACE,
AND HE LOOKED AROUND AND SAID:
I'M LONELY—
I'LL MAKE ME A WORLD. . . .

THEN GOD SMILED,
AND THE LIGHT BROKE.
AND THE DARKNESS ROLLED UP ON ONE SIDE,
AND THE LIGHT STOOD SHINING ON THE OTHER,
AND GOD SAID: THAT'S GOOD![8]

James Weldon Johnson was one of the earliest poets to win fame during the Harlem Renaissance.

The Johnson home in Harlem became a center for the literary and theater people of New York. It was not unusual to find the most prominent people in New York, both black and white, at one of Johnson's evening parties.

In 1927, Johnson published *God's Trombones*, a fictional series of seven sermons by an African-American preacher. The sermons were composed in a free-verse style. They used the rhythms, imagination, and feelings of traditional Southern African-American preachers. The sermons contained simple yet powerful language:

And now, O Lord—
When I've done drunk my last cup of sorrow—
When I've been called everything but a child of God
When I'm done travelling up the rough side of

the mountain—
O—Mary's Baby—
When I start down the steep and slippery steps of
death—
When this old world begins to rock beneath my feet—
Lower me to my dusty grave in peace
To wait for that great gittin' up morning.[9]

The work was instantly recognized as an important contribution to the establishment of a new African-American literature. The work inspired many other African-American artists to concentrate on African-American themes.

Claude McKay

After World War I, more African Americans began to achieve success as writers, getting their work published as books or in magazines with large circulations. Writers wanted to help build a positive self-image for African Americans and share the hope for the bright future they felt themselves.

One of the first African-American writers to achieve widespread notice was Claude McKay. Born in Jamaica in 1890, he had published two books of poetry there before he came to the United States to attend college. He spent one semester at Tuskegee Institute in Alabama and then transferred to Kansas State University. During the Great Migration, he moved to Harlem. He married and opened a restaurant, which soon failed. His wife went back to Jamaica with their child.

McKay remained in Harlem and went back to writing. To buy food and pay his bills, he worked as a waiter and dishwasher. But he devoted every moment he could to his writing. He sent his poems to many magazines. Eventually, McKay's poem "Harlem Dancer" was published. Some date the beginning of the Harlem Renaissance to the publication of this poem. Others push the date back another year, to 1919, when McKay's poem "If We Must Die" was published. "If We Must Die" is a call for African Americans to fight against racial prejudice and discrimination. In the strongest language, McKay tells African Americans:

> *If we must die, let it not be like hogs*
> *Hunted and penned in an inglorious spot,*
> *While round us bark the mad and hungry dogs,*
> *Making their mock at our accursed lot.*
> *If we must die, o, let us nobly die. . .* [10]

Regardless of the exact date the Harlem Renaissance began, one can sense in McKay's works a new attitude, a new joy, a new strength in being African-American. It was an attitude shared by almost all of his Harlem contemporaries.

Langston Hughes

Langston Hughes was born in Joplin, Missouri, in 1902. His parents were divorced when he was a child, and he went to live with his grandmother until he was twelve years old. He then moved to Lincoln, Illinois,

Langston Hughes became one of the most famous writers of the Harlem Renaissance.

to live with his mother and her second husband. He began to write poetry while he was in high school. After graduating, Hughes traveled to Mexico and talked his father into giving him the money to go to college. He was accepted to Columbia University in New York City, just a few blocks away from Harlem. After a year at Columbia, Hughes traveled to Africa and Europe. He returned to the United States and moved to Harlem in November 1924.

His poetic talent was acclaimed with the publication of his first poem, "The Negro Speaks of Rivers," in the June 1921 issue of *The Crisis*. Hughes's poem unites African Americans through all eternity, just as the rivers of the world are united in the world's oceans, and the blood of the body is united in the heart:

> *I've known rivers:*
> *I've known rivers ancient as the world*
> *and older than the flow*
> *of human blood in human veins.*
> *My soul has grown deep like the rivers*
> *I bathed in the Euphrates when dawns were young.*
> *I built my hut near the Congo and it lulled me to sleep*
> *I looked upon the Nile and raised the pyramids above it.*
> *I heard the singing of the Mississippi when Abe Lincoln went*
> *down to New Orleans, and I've seen its muddy bosom turn*
> *all golden in the sunset.*
> *I've known rivers:*
> *Ancient, dusky rivers.*
> *My soul has grown deep like the rivers.*[11]

In 1926, Hughes's first book of poetry, *The Weary Blues*, was published by the prestigious New York publisher Alfred A. Knopf. The book was a collection of poems that reflected Hughes's love of jazz, the popular music of the streets and speakeasies—the illegal bars found throughout New York during Prohibition. Hughes liked to write about the working-class people of the day, including jazz musicians, laborers, and street hustlers. The title poem shows Hughes's fine ear for the sounds of the common man:

Droning a drowsy syncopated tune,
Rocking back and forth to a mellow croon,
*   I heard a Negro play.*
Down on Lenox Avenue the other night
By the pale dull pallor of an old gas light
*   He did a lazy sway . . .*
*   He did a lazy sway . . .*
To the tune o' those Weary Blues.
With his ebony hands on each ivory key
He made that poor piano moan with melody.
*   O Blues!*
Swaying to and fro on his rickety stool
He played that sad raggy tune like a musical fool.
*   Sweet Blues!*
Coming from a black man's soul. . .[12]

For the next forty years, Hughes would produce more than sixty books of poetry, drama, opera, fiction, and nonfiction. His autobiography, *The Big Sea*, was published in 1940. Throughout his career, Hughes was applauded for his realistic portrayal of African-American life in the United States. He refused to make the African-American experience overly sad or overly sweet. He told it as he saw it. He died in 1967.

Opportunity

In 1923, the first issue of *Opportunity: A Journal of Negro Life* was published by the Urban League. Edited by Charles S. Johnson, *Opportunity* was first an organ for the political aims of the Urban League, but it also included fiction and poetry. It sponsored literary

SOURCE DOCUMENT

WHAT HAPPENS TO A DREAM DEFERRED?
DOES IT DRY UP
LIKE A RAISIN IN THE SUN?
OR FESTER LIKE A SORE—
AND THEN RUN? . . .[13]

Langston Hughes is one of the best-known poets of the Harlem Renaissance. This is an excerpt from his poem "A Dream Deferred."

contests through which many African Americans started their literary careers.

Special "Negro Issues" were also appearing in several national magazines that were entirely devoted to the talents of the new writers from Harlem. It was not only by chance that the literary explosion in Harlem was being recognized by the white mainstream. Many unrecognized black businessmen actively supported black artists and introduced their works to their white business associates.[14]

In November 1924, *Opportunity* magazine sponsored a dinner at the Harlem Civic Club. The dinner was held to celebrate the publication of a novel called *There is Confusion* by Jessie Fauset. Charles S. Johnson, James Weldon Johnson, and W.E.B. DuBois invited influential white editors, writers, and publishers to attend to meet some of the best new artists from Harlem.

One of those invited was Paul Kellogg, a white editor of the prestigious magazine *Survey*, whose audience included major philanthropists and social reformers. These people controlled a great deal of money and influence. If these men and women were informed about and interested in the explosion of African-American creativity in Harlem, they could direct a great deal of money to African-American causes.

Kellogg was very impressed with the people he met, just as DuBois and the others had hoped. In 1925, Kellogg invited Alain Locke, an African-American philosophy professor he had met at the *Opportunity* dinner, to edit a special issue of *Survey* that would be devoted to Harlem. Locke was then the only African American ever to have received the prestigious Rhodes scholarship, which pays for Americans to study at Oxford University in England.[15]

He invited a wide range of people of all ages and social and professional standings to contribute to this special issue of *Survey*. It was a great success. In the next issue, the *Survey* editors ran a long series of testimonials from those who were impressed with the cultural strides African Americans had recently been making.

The New Negro

Soon, Alain Locke arranged the *Survey* articles into book form. He titled the work *The New Negro*. The first part of the book was devoted to examples of the new African-American culture, including essays about art, fiction, poetry, drama, and music. A second part included academic essays by social scientists on the African-American experience in a big-city environment. A third section was a bibliography, a list of all the important books African Americans had already published.

Locke tried to convince his intended audience—mainly white businessmen and scholars—that the Harlem Renaissance showed how quickly African Americans had progressed after leaving the rural environment of the South and migrating to the large industrial cities of the North. The Great Migration had created a "New Negro":

> With this renewed self-respect and self-dependence, the life of the Negro community is bound to enter a new dynamic phase, the buoyancy from within compensating for whatever pressure there may be of conditions from without. The migrant masses, shifting from countryside to city, hurdle several generations of experience at a leap, but more important, the same thing happens spiritually in the life-attitudes and self-expression of the Young Negro, in his poetry, his art, his education and his new outlook, with the additional advantage, of course, of the poise and greater certainty of knowing what it is all about. From this comes the promise and warrant of a new leadership.[16]

Some writers, including some of those who had contributed to it, protested that the "New Negro" of the title was really a stereotype of what the white man wanted the black man to become, not a picture of the actual black experience. *The New Negro* may not have been a comprehensive picture of the reality of Harlem, but it did portray the new attitude of joy and optimism in being African-American that fueled the Harlem Renaissance. Harlem was quickly earning a national reputation as the center of a new and exciting freedom for young African-American artists. Many talented individuals were drawn there, not all of them ready to conform to the ideals of the "New Negro." Some found great treasures in the past that they wanted to preserve. Among these people was Zora Neale Hurston.

Zora Neale Hurston

Zora Neale Hurston was born on January 7, 1901, in Notasulga, Alabama. She moved to Eatonville, Florida, an all-African-American town, when she was still a baby. Her father, John, was a carpenter and preacher. He was a well-respected man in the town and was elected mayor several times. Her mother, Lucy, died when Zora was only three years old.

Eatonville was a township that had been created after the Civil War to give a home to former slaves. In Zora's early childhood, she became familiar with many old tales, songs, and traditions of the former slaves. She left home at the age of fourteen to work as a maid with a traveling theater company. She soon settled in Baltimore, Maryland, and enrolled at Morgan College Preparatory School. After graduating, she entered Howard University in Washington, D.C., in

Zora Neale Hurston rose from a modest background to become one of the best-known writers in America.

1920. She attended classes for the next four years and supported herself by working as a manicurist.

Zora Neale Hurston published her first story in the Howard University literary magazine in 1921.[17] In December 1924, *Opportunity* magazine published her story "Drenched in Light," and she came to the attention of other artists of the Harlem Renaissance. Encouraged by this success, Hurston moved to New York. She would later claim that she arrived with just $1.50 in her pocket.

In May 1925, she won a prize in a literary contest for her short story "Spunk."[18] Charles S. Johnson, the editor of *Opportunity*, recognized her great talent and

SOURCE DOCUMENT

BUT JOE KANTY NEVER CAME BACK, NEVER. THE MEN IN THE STORE HEARD THE SHARP REPORT OF A PISTOL SOMEWHERE DISTANT IN THE PALMETTO THICKET AND SOON SPUNK CAME WALKING LEISURELY, WITH HIS BIG BLACK STETSON SET AT THE SAME RAKISH ANGLE AND LENA CLINGING TO HIS ARM, CAME WALKING RIGHT INTO THE GENERAL STORE. LENA WEPT IN A FRIGHTENED MANNER.

"WELL," SPUNK ANNOUNCED CALMLY, "JOE COME OUT THERE WID A MEAT AXE AN' MADE ME KILL HIM."[19]

An excerpt from Zora Neale Hurston's award-winning short story "Spunk."

became her friend and supporter. The Johnson family often had Hurston to their home for dinner, and Johnson often helped her with money for expenses. In 1925, she received a scholarship to Barnard College, the women's division of Columbia University. There, she studied anthropology under Franz Boaz, one of the first people to teach that the folktales—including Zora Neale Hurston's stories from her youth—were valuable and should be shared with the rest of the world. In January 1926, "John Redding Goes to Sea" was published in *Opportunity*.

Fire!

In 1926, Zora Neale Hurston, Langston Hughes, and other African-American artists who were not pleased with the picture of the African-American experience that was depicted in Alain Locke's *The New Negro*, founded a new magazine. They named it *Fire!* Hughes said they chose that title because "it would burn up a lot of the old, dead conventional Negro-white writers and artists."[20] He used the term *Negro-white* to indicate that he thought black writers and artists of the past too often had imitated white styles, seeking to impress whites, rather than searching for their own black voices.

The first issue of *Fire!* appeared in November 1926. It included a wide variety of pieces. Many of them seemed radical. Hurston contributed a story called "Sweat." Hughes included a poem called "Elevator Boy" that began, "I got a job now / runnin' an elevator. . . ."[21] He had begun writing more and more like he heard African Americans speak. Countee Cullen's poem for the issue was worded more like a famous white poet's might be, but it had a bitter tone, describing the suffering of a black writer in a white society.

Fire! did not sell well. African-American literary critics, who were more in tune with the ideals of *The New Negro*, hated it. They did not recommend it in their newspaper and magazine columns. Then, ironically, hundreds of copies burned in a fire. A second issue never appeared.[22]

The Literary Life

An extraordinary number of writers continued to live and work in Harlem during the late 1920s. Individuals came to Harlem, stayed a while, and left. Some, like

Taken in 1922, this photograph shows two men sharing a book. Harlem Renaissance works often became popular when they were passed among friends.

Claude McKay, moved on to Europe. Others, like Jean Toomer, lost interest in writing. But new writers continued to arrive all the time, inspired by those whose works they had read back home in the South or West.

Almost all African-American writers were published in African-American magazines and newspapers in Harlem, but many also sent their work to white publishers. Some were able to support themselves through writing. Having published one or two works, they found themselves "adopted" by editors or publishers who eagerly read their new writing, accepted it, and even placed orders for more. Others did not achieve this level of success. They sold less and their income was less regular. Some threw rent parties to pay the bills. Others worked at a job during the day and wrote only in their spare time. Writing was their love but not necessarily their profession.

Writers' Interaction

Most writers of the Harlem Renaissance knew each other. They formed study groups.[23] Some formed friendships. They sometimes joined to put out a small magazine or journal. The younger, radical writers often saw each other in bars and clubs and at rent parties. Members of the older generation went to publishers' parties, openings of exhibitions at art galleries, and book signings. Novelist Jessie Fauset, who was also literary editor of *Opportunity*, invited many writers and other creative people to her home. A rich African-American heiress named A'lelia Walker invited all kinds of celebrities to her apartment. She liked to introduce writers, artists, musicians, editors, and publishers to businesspeople and politicians. Both black and white people crowded her parties.

The Harlem Renaissance was not just a time for writers. Artists of all kinds intermingled and helped each other create. Graphic artists worked alongside writers to produce art for their magazines, sets for their stage plays, and illustrations and covers for their books. African-American musicians composed serious operas and classical music. But, just like today and probably always, the most popular musicians created their music for the common people. Harlem was alive with music coming from the clubs and the streets.

MUSIC AND THE THEATER

One of the first African-American composers of opera was Harry Lawrence Freeman. His first work, *The Martyr*, was the first opera ever produced by an all-African-American company. He wrote a series of three operas on the theme of Zulu (an African people) history. In September 1928, his opera *Voodoo* opened at the 52nd Street Theater in New York. In the spring of 1930, it was performed at Steinway Hall.[1]

Freeman composed music in other forms, too. He wrote "The Slave" as a poem to be accompanied by an orchestra. In addition to composing, Freeman taught music and opened his own music school for training in opera.[2]

Another African-American classical musician of the period was Roland Hayes. Hayes was the son of a slave from Georgia, who had received his training at Fisk University in Nashville. He later toured with the Fisk Jubilee Singers. After leaving school, Hayes arranged for his own concert tours. He traveled to Europe and sang for the king and queen of England.

In 1923, Hayes returned to the United States and gave his debut American concert at Town Hall in New York. He was generous with his time and often gave both money and instruction to aspiring singers.

The History of Ragtime, Blues, and Jazz

It is not for its contributions to classical music that the Harlem Renaissance is noted today, however. The music of the Harlem Renaissance that remains alive and vibrant today is the purely African-American styles of music created in the South that came to Harlem along with the thousands of new migrants. It was the music of the dance clubs and the speakeasies. It was the music of the street. Parts of it came from the lonely, sad songs of slaves—the music of the slave without freedom, of the African-American man without a job, of the African-American woman without her child. It was sad music, but it did not make listeners cry. It made people strong, made them laugh, made them move to the strong and rhythmic beat of the guitar.

The blues, as this music is called, has been sung for more than two hundred years.[3] It was a long time before it was recognized in published form. Even though these songs were hardly ever written down, many African-American musicians knew them.

Another type of African-American music was ragtime. Rag was a quick piano style that produced a highly infectious tune. It was great for dancing.

Ragtime was hugely influenced by one man. In 1899, Scott Joplin, from Texas, convinced a music

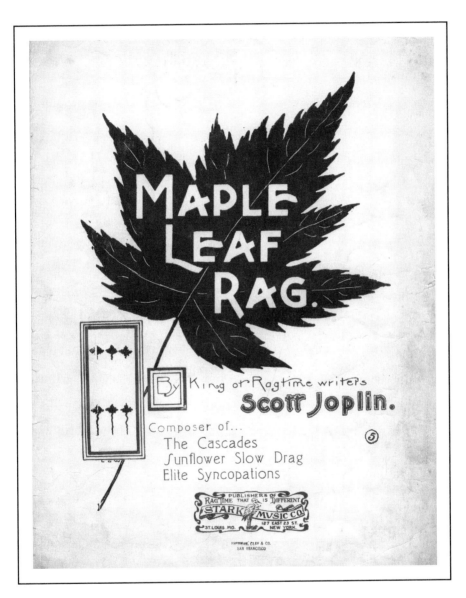

Scott Joplin's "Maple Leaf Rag" earned the composer a lot of money. Joplin was the primary influence on ragtime music.

publisher to give him a penny for each copy of his new "Maple Leaf Rag" that was sold. That contract gave Joplin a nice income for the rest of his life. Sales the first year were only four hundred copies. By 1909, however, approximately five hundred thousand copies had been sold. Sales of the song continued at such a fevered pace for the next twenty years.

Joplin was a master of ragtime, composing hundreds of "rags." Ragtime soon became America's most popular music. Ragtime music was upbeat, catchy, toe-tapping music. It used syncopated rhythms—very hard to play—that refused to allow anyone to feel sad during its playing. Ragtime became popular in the bars and dance halls of the South and spread north as African Americans moved into industrial cities like Chicago and New York.[4]

Jazz was born soon after the blues and ragtime. It combined the two forms and gave great freedom to the musicians, who played in bars and restaurants in small bands. Each musician in the band would change the basic melody or rhythm of the tune when it became his turn to play his solo. It was the job of the other musicians to recognize the changes and to play along. Jazz was music for experts—not necessarily experts trained in concert halls, but those who knew the tunes and limits of their instruments and the minds and hearts of the other musicians.

Jazz was exciting. It drew huge audiences to very small clubs when noted musicians were set to appear. In the 1920s, jazz became extremely popular in both

Chicago and New York, especially in Harlem. Members of the older generation of African-American leaders, such as Alain Locke and W.E.B. DuBois, did not set much stock in blues or jazz. Many of the writers and artists of the Harlem Renaissance, however, loved the new music. They found it inspiring. Many white Americans agreed.

Blues and Jazz in the 1920s

Blues records began to sell in great numbers around 1920. That was the first time any recorded African-American music had sold well. The biggest blues stars of the early years were women. Mamie Smith's "Crazy Blues," recorded for a white-owned record label in New York in 1920, set records when it sold seventy-five thousand copies in one month.[5] She had sold a million copies at the end of six months. Victoria Spivey, Bessie Smith, Ethel Waters, and Ida Cox were other African-American women who hit it big.

But jazz was the most popular music of the 1920s. In fact, the decade is often referred to as the Jazz Age. Jazz was played all over Harlem. Some musicians became world famous as they played in clubs all over the United States and Europe. Thanks to the development of records and, soon, the radio, their sounds reached even farther.

Musicians practiced at home and on street corners. They played at rent parties. Nightclubs abounded. The most famous included the Roseland, the Savoy Ballroom, and the Cotton Club.

Louis Armstrong remains one of the best-known musicians of the jazz world.

Fletcher Henderson was the band leader at the Roseland.[6] In 1924, Henderson paid for a young cornet player named Louis Armstrong to come to Harlem from Chicago to join his band. An orphan, Armstrong had lived as a child on the streets of New Orleans until he was placed in a African-American orphanage called the Colored Waifs' Home. There, he joined a brass band. As soon as he could leave the home, at age sixteen, he became a professional jazz musician, playing in a large number of bands. He was twenty-four years old when he started to work for Henderson. A year later, he was leading his own jazz band.

The Savoy Ballroom was a nightclub the residents of Harlem loved to frequent. People from all walks of life and of all races went there to drink illegal alcoholic beverages, listen to music, and dance. In fact, many popular dances of the 1920s, such as the Lindy, the Shimmy, and the Suzy-Q, were first developed at the Savoy.[7] Other clubs, however, were not the apparent "melting pot" of music fans that the Savoy was. Many of the most popular jazz clubs of the time had strict rules about segregation. Although African Americans were, of course, the featured entertainers, many clubs refused admittance to African Americans who hoped to be part of the audience.

Duke Ellington

One world-class musician who rose to fame with the music of Harlem was big-band leader Duke Ellington. Ellington belonged to a middle-class African-American family from Washington, D.C. His father became a policeman—a notable achievement for an African-American man in his day. In 1923, at age twenty-four, Ellington moved to Harlem. A ragtime piano player, he aspired to become a bandleader. He started playing in small clubs. Slowly he achieved his goal, gaining a reputation as a great musician.

Ellington formed a large orchestra of thirty or forty musicians. It was called a big band, to distinguish it from the much smaller jazz band. Big bands were not the place for musicians who wanted to improvise.

Duke Ellington was among the first musicians to utilize the big-band sound.

Most of the creativity of big bands came in the form of arrangements for the whole orchestra that were written by the bandleader. Most big bands developed their own styles and were instantly recognizable to their many fans who saw them or listened to them on the radio. Duke Ellington's band gained a good reputation and started to appear in Harlem's ritzier establishments. By 1927, Duke Ellington's orchestra was appearing nightly at the Cotton Club. Radio soon won Ellington a national audience.

For a long time, African-American leaders spurned the jazz men. They did not see Ellington as an example of the "New Negro." They wanted African-American musicians and composers to gain fame writing and playing classical symphonies and operas, not jazz. Despite their disapproval, jazz has lived on to become the only art form to be born in the United States. Today, around the world, people study these outcasts of the "New Negro" movement as true geniuses of American art.[8]

Black Musicals

On May 22, 1921, an all-African-American musical, *Shuffle Along*, written by Noble Sissle and Eubie Blake, appeared at the David Belasco Theater on Broadway. It was an instant success. Josephine Baker and Florence Mills were some of the talented cast members.[9] Florence Mills became tremendously famous and went to London, where she made another huge sensation. African Americans admired her not just for her voice,

SOURCE DOCUMENT

"FLORENCE MILLS KNOCKED 'EM DEAD EV'VY TIME SHE CAME ON THE STAGE. THE DUKE A WIN'SOR (THEN HE WAS THE PRINCE OF WALES) SAW HER 'STRUT HER STUFF' THIRTEEN TIMES. THEY EVEN CALL HER THE NEGRO AMBASSADOR TO THE WORLD, BUT THINGS LIKE THAT NEVER WENT TO HER HEAD. HER SPIRIT WAS TYPICAL OF THE NEGRO, AND DID SHE HAVE PRIDE IN HER PEOPLE! ..."[10]

This is an excerpt from an interview with an African-American former dancing girl, describing the fame of dancer Florence Mills.

but because she made the astronomical sum of $3,500 per week.[11]

Throughout the 1920s, African-American musicals continued to draw large audiences at white theaters in New York and the rest of the country. *From Dixie to Broadway, Blackbirds of 1928, Blackberries, Rang Tang, Chocolate Dandies,* and *Running Wild* were some of the most popular.[12]

Theater

During the Harlem Renaissance, African-American artists, many of them women, helped create a serious forum for African-American drama both in small theaters in Harlem and on the larger Broadway stage—before mostly white audiences. In the 1920s, five serious African-American dramas, written by and about African Americans, played on the Broadway stage. These plays presented African-American themes and social problems directly to many members of the white audience for the first time.

Angelina Weld Grimké was one of the earliest African-American dramatists. She was born in 1880 in Boston, Massachusetts. Her father was Archibald Grimké, a prominent journalist who was an official of the NAACP. Angelina was educated in Massachusetts and Minnesota and became an English teacher in Washington, D.C., in 1907. She wrote poetry and plays.

Angelina Grimké's first play, *Rachael*, was first presented by the NAACP at the Myrtill School in Washington. It was published in 1920 in book form. She wrote it "to enlighten the American people relative to the lamentable condition of the millions of Colored citizens in this free republic."[13]

Rachael is a play of outrage at the racial bigotry of the day, modeled in many ways on the life and feelings of its author. Rachael Loving, the heroine of the play, refuses to get married or have children because the destructive effect of racism makes the lives of African-American children too horrible. She dreams of unborn African-American children coming to her in her sleep, begging not to be born into such a world. The play ends as Rachael cries to her unborn children,

> I shall never see you now. Your little, brown, beautiful bodies—I shall never see. Your dimples—everywhere— your laughter—your tears—the beautiful, lovely feel of you here (puts her hands against her heart) Never— never—to be.[14]

Other important African-American women dramatists of the Harlem Renaissance include Alice Dunbar-Nelson, Mary Burrill, Myrtle Smith Livingston, Ruth Gainers-Shelton, and Eulalie Spence. Between 1918 and 1930, eleven African-American women dramatists published a total of twenty-one plays. Some of these were not produced on a stage, but most were performed locally in Harlem at small theaters, churches, and meeting halls.

Willis Richardson, another important African-American dramatist of the Harlem Renaissance, later wrote an article printed in *The Crisis*, "The Hope of the Negro Drama." In it, he noted the ways a dramatist could approach the topic of being African-American. He wrote,

> Rachel is a propaganda play and a great portion of it shows the manner in which Negroes are treated by white people in the United States. Still there is another kind of play: the kind that shows the soul of the people; and the soul of this people is truly worth showing.[15]

In a career of over thirty years, Willis Richardson wrote forty-eight plays on a wide variety of themes. He wrote plays for children, plays on African-American historical figures, and plays on everyday themes of family and marriage. Richardson's first play, *The Deacon's Awakening,* which supported equal rights for women, was inspired by *Rachael*. It was published in *The Crisis* in 1920.

W.E.B. DuBois encouraged Richardson to ask Raymond O'Neil, the director of the Ethiopian Art Players in Chicago, to produce his plays on stage. O'Neil's company took another Richardson play, *The Chip Woman's Fortune*, and produced it first in Chicago and then at the Frazee Theater in New York in May 1923. *The Chip Woman's Fortune* was the first serious drama, not a musical, written by an African American to be produced on Broadway. It was a one-act play that demonstrated an African-American family's ability to overcome the social and economic problems of the times, mainly through the wisdom and patience of the oldest member of the family, Aunt Nancy. Aunt Nancy represented the traditional mother of African culture whose strength, dedication, and love keep the family together. In some ways, it is the answer to the despair of *Rachael*—that the loving family can overcome problems a single person cannot.

Garland Anderson's play *Appearances* was the first full-length play—three acts—written by an African-American man to appear on Broadway. Garland, who had no formal training in literature and had gone no further than the fourth grade, was inspired to write when a friend gave him a free ticket to see a stage play. He wrote *Appearances* in three weeks. The play opened at the Frolic Theater on October 13, 1925. It ran for twenty-three performances. It is the story of Carl, a bellhop, who is falsely accused by a white woman of rape. It was a controversial theme for the stage at that time. The play toured the country, giving performances in Los Angeles, Seattle, Chicago, and San Francisco between 1927 and 1929, before it returned to New York. In 1930, it went overseas to London.

Many Harlem dramatists were writing novels and poems at the same time they wrote plays. Langston Hughes wrote more than thirty plays and operas, including *Mule Bone* in 1932 with Zora Neale Hurston, and *Mulatto* in 1935. Many writers wrote plays intended not for Broadway but instead for a home audience.

The Krigwa Players was an all-African-American theatrical group. They had their stage in the basement of the 135th Street branch of the public library. They described their purpose as "An Attempt to establish in High Harlem, New York City, a little Theatre which shall be primarily a center where Negro actors before Negro audiences interpret Negro life as depicted by Negro artists."[16]

The cost of the Krigwa Players' informal theater shows was probably nothing or just a donation. The scenery was produced by the company as cheaply as possible, and anyone who wanted to act could join the company. It was truly a community theater. It gave all members of the Harlem community a chance experience the joys of theater.[17]

ART

Many opportunities were open to African-American artists during the 1920s. Some sold drawings or prints to magazines. As the decade went on, painters and sculptors found more places to display their art. Galleries also held shows of works by African-American artists.

In 1921, the Harlem branch of the New York Public Library held an exhibition of artworks by African-American artists. Some of the best known African-American artists of the time, including Henry Tanner, Laura Wheeler Waring, W. E. Scott, Meta Fuller, and W. E. Braxton, displayed their works there. These artists were already recognized by the art community, and their works sold for a good price.

At the same time, there were hundreds of aspiring young artists, many of whom had no formal training, who were moving into Harlem. These people got jobs to support themselves, but devoted all their spare time to expressing their creative urges in new styles that showed the new African-American pride and optimism.

Sculptor Augusta Savage struggled for a long time to be noticed. She came to New York City from Palm

Beach, Florida, in 1920, with $4.60 in her pocket. The Cooper Union, a famous free art school, accepted her, but she had to work at a series of poorly paying jobs before she sold enough sculptures to pay her bills. Eventually, she received important commissions. She was hired, for example, to create busts of W.E.B. DuBois and Marcus Garvey.

Some of the best art that came out of the Harlem Renaissance included the small printed signs and advertisements that were posted on telephone poles and buildings of Harlem throughout the 1920s. Most of these works of art were torn down and thrown away as trash once the dance or rent party or theater performance they advertised was over. Any of these posters that still exist today are displayed in museums and treasured by collectors. Most of this poster work was done by struggling African-American artists of the neighborhood. There were plenty of young artists who came to Harlem from all over the United States for the freedom of expression and the exciting lifestyle the neighborhood offered. Often, these artists would paint a poster or carve a woodcut design for an advertisement just to gain free admission or as a favor for a friend. Only a few of these struggling artists remain famous today. One of the most important was Aaron Douglas.

Aaron Douglas

Aaron Douglas was born in Topeka, Kansas, on May 26, 1899. In 1922, he graduated from the University of Nebraska with a degree in fine arts. His first job was teaching drawing at Lincoln High School in Kansas City, Missouri. He quickly learned that he wanted to create art, not teach it. He moved to Harlem in 1924.[1]

Shortly after his arrival, Douglas met the noted German-American artist Winold Reiss. Reiss noted that Douglas was a good technical artist, but he encouraged Douglas to abandon the more conventional styles of the times. Instead, Reiss encouraged Douglas to develop his own African-American art based on the ancestral designs and geometric patterns of ancient African art. This style came to be called geometric symbolism.

From Alain Locke, a friend and employer of Reiss, Douglas was exposed to the growing collections of African art that were being assembled in American museums and galleries. Locke chose Douglas to make the black-and-white woodcuts that were to be used as illustrations between the chapters of the March 1925 edition of *The New Negro*.[2] Alain Locke included his essay, "The Legacy of the Ancestral Arts," in *The New Negro*. The essay called for African-American artists, like Douglas, to continue the strong and vital tradition of African sculpture in their quest to find a truly African-American style. Locke recognized that the sculptural art of Africa had inspired the art of such leading modern artists in Europe as Pablo Picasso and Constantine Brancusi. He felt that such roots could serve as the foundation of a great African-American art.

Douglas quickly became one of the most influential artists of the Harlem Renaissance. Locke called him a pioneer of African-American art. Douglas's art was an immediate success. In 1925, he illustrated the cover of *Opportunity* magazine and was awarded the magazine's first prize for excellence in art. He also received the first prize from *The Crisis* magazine for his illustration "The African Chieftain." W.E.B. DuBois encouraged Douglas to become a regular contributor to *The Crisis* and other periodicals. In 1926, Douglas and Richard Bruce Nugent illustrated and helped produce the short-lived magazine *Fire!*

Critics found Douglas's work refreshing and new. Douglas's works were simple. He used geometric shapes such as circles, triangles, and squares as a strong background for the silhouettes of African Americans which formed the core of the work. Douglas's reputation quickly spread to the mainstream white publications. His works soon appeared in *Vanity Fair* and *Theater Arts Monthly.*

He became even busier in 1927. He completed his first mural, "Fire!," on the walls of the Club Ebony in Harlem. He also illustrated several well-known books and magazines.

In 1929, Douglas began to paint two murals, one for the Erasto Milo Cravath Library at Fisk University in Nashville, Tennessee, and the other for the Sherman Hotel in Chicago, Illinois. Both murals depict strong, joyful images of African Americans. These works mark

Weary As I Can Be

Artist Aaron Douglas produced this woodcut for the October 1926 issue of Opportunity.

the beginning of a series of works known as his Hallelujah period.

Another artist who was inspired by the depths of African heritage and loved the simplicity and strength of African images was Palmer Hayden.

Palmer Hayden

Peyton Cole Hedgeman was born in Wide Water, Virginia, on January 15, 1890. In 1914, Peyton joined the army and served in the Philippines and at the United States Military Academy at West Point. During his enlistment, his name was changed to Palmer Hayden by a commanding sergeant who could not pronounce his name correctly.

Hayden arrived in New York City in 1919 and began a series of jobs that included mailman, house cleaner, and porter while he studied art at Cooper Union. Palmer demonstrated his talent in several styles, winning $400 and the first-place medal for his watercolor of the Portland, Maine, waterfront at the first Harmon Foundation exhibition of African-American art in 1926.

Hayden changed styles the same year in his oil painting "Fetiche et Fleurs." It shows a Fang mask from Gabon and a Bakuba raffia cloth from the Congo.[3] This unconventional still-life showed Hayden's growing preference for themes dealing with his African heritage.

In 1927, Hayden received a $3,000 grant from a private sponsor to live and paint in Europe. For the next five years, Hayden remained in Europe and began a series of works that showed the heroes and stories of African-American history. His works were displayed in both Europe and the United States. He returned to the United States in 1932.

In 1944, Hayden began a series of twelve paintings about the legend of John Henry that took him ten years to finish. Hayden continued to paint and display his works almost until the end of his life. He died on February 18, 1973, at the age of eighty-three.[4]

James Van Der Zee

Both Aaron Douglas and Palmer Hayden developed powerful symbolic styles to show the African-American identity and heritage. James Van Der Zee used no symbolism. His artistic outlet was his camera. With it, Van Der Zee created a large and beautiful picture of life as it really was in Harlem during the 1920s.

Van Der Zee was born on June 29, 1886, in Lennox, Massachusetts. He grew up in New England in a happy home. Early in his life, he demonstrated a love of music and art. He began to take photographs in his early teens. In 1905, he moved to New York City and supported himself with jobs as an elevator operator and musician. He was a good baseball player, but he chose photography as a profession after being hit in the head a couple of times. Van Der Zee learned to develop photographs at a portrait photographer's studio in Newark, New Jersey, in 1915. He quickly developed a reputation as a fine portrait photographer.

This Harlem family posed for photographer James Van Der Zee in 1925.

In 1916, he opened the Guarantee Photo Studio in Harlem on West 135th Street. For the next forty years, he took   pictures of thousands of Harlem residents who came to his studio and paid a small fee.[5] UNIA, founded by Marcus Garvey, named him its official photographer, and hundreds of his photographs of UNIA activities appeared in African-American newspapers across the United States.[6] Van Der Zee also photographed the neighborhood people on the streets and at funerals, weddings, and parades. He captured the daily life of Harlem. His portraits reveal a people who took a great deal of pride in their appearance. The vast majority of his candid photographs show happy, smiling people.

Van Der Zee continued to artfully depict African-American life in Harlem and New York well into the 1960s and 1970s. His work documents how people faced the burdens of the Great Depression, World War II, and the civil rights movement of the 1950s and 1960s. A portrait by James Van Der Zee is considered a family heirloom today, although Van Der Zee often charged just a dollar for his work during the Harlem Renaissance.

7

THE END OF THE HARLEM RENAISSANCE

The joyous world of Harlem—and the rest of the United States—changed dramatically on October 29, 1929. History books refer to that day as Black Tuesday. All through the 1920s, Americans had generally enjoyed great prosperity. Many people had borrowed a great deal of money and invested it in the stock market. Stock prices had risen steadily. There was a feeling that the United States was making great progress and that its strides would just continue to become greater. But in reality, big segments of the American economy were in trouble. Few Americans realized that industry was declining at the end of the decade. The Federal Reserve Board warned of trouble ahead. It advised bankers not to lend money for people to play the stock market. Seemingly, no one paid attention—that is, until the stock market crashed.

Many stocks plummeted in value until they were worth almost nothing. It was the beginning of an economic depression that affected the entire world and lasted more than ten years.

SOURCE DOCUMENT

AGONIZING SCENES WERE ENACTED IN THE CUSTOMERS' ROOMS OF VARIOUS BROKERS. THERE TRADERS WHO A FEW DAYS BEFORE HAD LUXURIATED IN DELUSION OF WEALTH SAW ALL THEIR HOPES SMASHED IN A COLLAPSE SO DEVASTATING, SO FAR BEYOND THEIR WILDEST FEARS, AS TO SEEM UNREAL. . . . THE EXCITEMENT AND SENSE OF DANGER WHICH IMBUED WALL STREET WAS LIKE THAT WHICH GRIPS MEN ON A SINKING SHIP. A CAMARADERIE, A KIND OF GAIETY OF DESPAIR, SPRANG UP. THE WALL STREET REPORTER FOUND ALL DOORS OPEN AND EVERYONE SNATCHED AT HIM FOR THE LATEST NEWS, FOR SHREDS OF RUMOUR. WHO WAS IN TROUBLE? WHO HAD GONE UNDER LAST? WHERE WAS IT GOING TO END?[1]

Elliott V. Bell described people's reactions to the stock market crash of October 1929.

The Great Depression would take an enormous toll on Americans. As banks closed, factories did, too. Unemployment soared. Farmers went bankrupt. Many families were left with no income at all. Men left their families and became hoboes, hopping trains to travel across the country, looking for work.[2]

African Americans and the Depression

Both rural and urban African Americans had a hard time during the 1930s. Many African-American sharecroppers were forced off their rented lands. African-American farmers were forced to sell their lands because they could no longer sell their crops for enough money to pay their land payments. Layoffs in businesses and industry were also widespread. The most unskilled laborers were laid off first. Of these, blacks were often laid off before their white contemporaries because of racial prejudice. There was fierce competition for the few jobs that did become available. Some unions fought to keep blacks out of their ranks, hoping to protect white workers from having to compete with blacks. Managers gave nonunion jobs to whites rather than African Americans because there was "a prevailing sentiment that Negroes should not be hired as long as there are white men without work," in the words of a 1936 study.[3]

In this climate of desperation and tension, African Americans were frequently victims of violence. Lynching continued. African Americans fought back against such discrimination and violence both as individuals and through organizations. African-American political groups changed their tactics. The NAACP went to court to file lawsuits in an attempt to fight racism. It also tried to persuade legislators to protect African-American rights. The Urban League organized boycotts by blacks of businesses that hired only white employees.

Decline of the Harlem Renaissance

The Depression brought the Harlem Renaissance to an end. African Americans in Harlem suffered and protested like those elsewhere. In 1935, a riot in

Harlem caused $200 million in property damage and resulted in three deaths.

The people of Harlem had to make do. Pushcart peddlers went around collecting and selling junk. People sold food from carts or stalls. To attract attention, some became street criers. They made up lyrics about their wares and sang them to popular tunes.[4]

African-American writers and other artists faced the same problems as African Americans in other lines of work. In the 1920s, many participants in the Harlem Renaissance had, from time to time, made ends meet by taking on menial jobs or throwing rent parties. After the Depression began, this was no longer possible. There were not enough jobs—even ones that paid poorly—to be found.

The Writer's Project

When Franklin Delano Roosevelt became president, he instituted the New Deal, a program of laws and federal aid designed to lift the country out of the Depression. Some African-American writers and artists found employment through the Works Progress Administration's (WPA) Writers Project, a New Deal program to make work for artists and writers. Throughout the country, these artists worked on projects that were intended to inform the public of its cultural heritage. African-American WPA writers in New York included Ralph Ellison, Dorothy West, and Zora Neale Hurston. They wrote stories about life in

Harlem, painted murals in government buildings, and did research on local history and social issues.

The creative life of Harlem did continue, but it was not as widely publicized as it had been during the height of the Harlem Renaissance. After the close of the WPA in the 1940s, there were fewer African-American artists than during the 1920s. Some writers from the Harlem Renaissance remained at work. Langston Hughes, for example, wrote until his death in the 1960s. Zora Neale Hurston wrote for another twenty years, doing some of her best work in the 1930s. But then she stopped. A journalist found her in the 1950s, living in poverty and doing odd jobs. Other leaders of the Harlem Renaissance also took up other lines of work. Their works went out of print. Photographer James Van Der Zee kept working for thirty more years, making memorable photographs of celebrities such as Louis Armstrong, but finally closed his studio in the 1950s.

A New Generation

A new generation of African-American writers set to work in the 1930s and 1940s. They had different ideas. Gradually, they would receive different recognition, too.

This generation's brightest light was Ralph Ellison. He wrote just one novel, *Invisible Man*. During the Harlem Renaissance, Alain Locke had tried to convince Americans that African Americans deserved recognition as thinking, creating achievers. His vision of black America was tied up with his hopes for a brilliant future. Ellison had a very different point of view. His title summed up his opinion—that the ordinary African-American man was invisible and did not count in American society. Black and white readers found *Invisible Man* very moving, despite the fact that it painted a harsh picture. It received the National Book Award in 1952, signaling that many critics thought it the most important piece of literature published that year.[5]

A new African-American consciousness came about in the 1960s. New African-American writers appeared in print. But older works were also being read again. By the time David Levering Lewis published *When Harlem Was in Vogue* in 1982,

> most of the literature of that time and place was reissued; scholars began to comb overlooked archives and private collections; books and dissertations appeared; conferences blossomed; and universities as well as high schools began to teach the writing of Jean Toomer, Claude McKay, Zora Neale Hurston, Countee Cullen, and Langston Hughes.[6]

Through the years of the civil rights movement and beyond, many other successful African-American writers became famous, including James Baldwin, Nikki Giovanni, Ishmael Reed, Toni Morrison, Maya Angelou, and Alice Walker. They all acknowledged a great debt to the Harlem Renaissance.[7]

In Harlem, celebrities would frequent the Hotel Theresa's Tap Room. During the Great Depression, however, Harlem businesses were hit hard by poor economic conditions.

What Happened to Harlem

Although some members of the Harlem Renaissance had refused to admit it, Harlem had social and economic problems even during the 1920s.[8] Basic difficulties like overcrowding and crime were allowed to grow during the Great Depression simply because there was no money to combat them. The neighborhood deteriorated. Buildings remained vacant. Slums grew. The crime rate soared. Still, Harlem remained a center for African-American spiritual, literary, and political involvement.[9] Well-known civil rights leader Malcolm X lived in Harlem. He headed the Harlem Mosque for the Nation of Islam and founded the Organization for African American Unity there in the early 1960s. David Dinkins was born in Harlem. In 1990, he became the first African American elected mayor of New York City.[10]

Today, cultural institutions in Harlem are at the forefront, celebrating African-American history and culture. One of these is the Schomburg Center for Research in Black Culture. Another is the National Black Theater. The Apollo Theater, an important center for African-American music, is also located in Harlem. Even today, despite its reputation as a dangerous, crime-ridden area, Harlem remains a center of African-American culture, history, and creativity.

8

THE LEGACY OF THE HARLEM RENAISSANCE

Most of the people involved in the day-to-day creativity in Harlem thought their work was significant. They liked being able to support themselves through their artistic efforts. They felt personal satisfaction when they achieved recognition for their work. They also had high hopes that their work would lead to great things, not just for themselves but for African Americans in general. Alain Locke hoped that the ideal of the "New Negro" would help African Americans win respect from the larger American population, both black and white. He thought that, one day, the achievements of the Harlem Renaissance would earn a respect that would reflect on the entire nation of African Americans.

The Reaction of Other African Americans

Locke's hopes did not seem realistic to some other members of the Harlem Renaissance or the African-American community. In fact, most African Americans paid the Harlem Renaissance little attention. The

This 1924 photograph shows an African-American couple enjoying the good life in Harlem.

African-American literary magazines of the Harlem Renaissance had only a small circulation. The books written by the famed African-American writers of the day did not make it into ordinary people's homes. Langston Hughes himself wrote that, "The ordinary Negroes hadn't heard of the Negro Renaissance. And if they had, it hadn't raised their wages any."[1]

Hughes's comment reveals the same truth that prompted Booker T. Washington to be accommodating while giving African Americans the means to achieve self-sufficiency: If African Americans did not have the economic means to join the middle class in America, they could never afford to buy books or have the leisure time to read them. They could not take classes or send their children to college. Racial equality could only follow some measure of economic equality. During the 1920s, just like whites, most blacks focused their attention on getting ahead in America. They were more concerned with their own earnings, their own way of life, than larger cultural causes.

The Influence of the Harlem Renaissance

African-American literature, art, and music were quickly recognized and applauded by the segment of white Americans who knew of the Harlem Renaissance. Although the number of these people was always small, they were living in New York, the hub of American business, communication, and culture. They had great influence and saw to it that the new African-American cultural flowering was absorbed into the general consciousness.[2]

Some Harlem Renaissance writings appeared only in publications intended for African-American audiences. But others were printed in general magazines and newspapers. Americans became aware that, in Harlem, there existed a group interested in the fine arts, creative literature, and classical music.[3]

White intellectuals and social activists became involved in trying to improve race relations. White publishers accepted some African-American writers' work. Some white people became patrons of talented artists.

Today, the Harlem Renaissance is not just a topic covered in standard American histories; it is considered an important enough subject to merit its own courses in colleges and universities.[4] Scholars publish several new books on the Harlem Renaissance every year. Historians express interest in the movement for many reasons: its significance in terms of African-American culture, its importance as a part of American literary history, and the insights it offers into the workings of a community of creativity.

One reason the Harlem Renaissance receives so much scholarly attention is because it raises issues for debate among historians. Some define the Harlem Renaissance narrowly, as a literary movement to which only writers contributed. Some count only fiction and poetry as works of the Harlem Renaissance. Others consider nonfiction pieces part of the Harlem Renaissance. Many other scholars see musicians, artists, and actors as part of the Harlem Renaissance. Writers like Langston Hughes and Zora Neale Hurston interacted with people involved in many creative endeavors. Both wrote about subjects like music. Hurston studied Negro spirituals. Hughes wrote poems that imitated jazz.

But the Harlem Renaissance is not just of interest to scholars. High-school history and English teachers include lessons on the Harlem Renaissance. It allows them to explore themes such as race relations.

In this photograph of a Harlem couple's wedding, the image of a little girl is superimposed in the lower left corner to show the predicted future for the young couple.

The Harlem Renaissance also fires the imagination of ordinary people. Americans, both black and white, often think fondly of the 1920s, because they seem like simpler and happier times. Americans still understand the forces that drew so many creative people to Harlem. The African-American community today celebrates its history. The Harlem Renaissance is among the topics most frequently covered in Black History Month (observed every year in February) events. Works of art, music, and literature from the Harlem Renaissance continue to be enjoyed by members of every new generation.

In February 1998, the California Palace of the Legion of Honor, a museum in San Francisco, mounted its *Rhapsodies in Black* exhibition. People flocked to this Harlem Renaissance exhibit. They talked excitedly as they read excerpts from magazines, got an up-close look at bright paintings, and listened to jazz recordings. The exhibit received national coverage on television and in magazines and newspapers. Curators reported that many visitors asked where they could find out more—where they could read, see, and listen to more works from that great cultural movement. Clearly, the Harlem Renaissance continues to resonate today.

★ TIMELINE ★

1658—Europeans build a settlement in what will later become Harlem.

1865—The Civil War ends.

1900—Booker T. Washington publishes his auto-biography; At the time, there are only a few other African-American authors, but there are many African-American newspapers; It is only around this time that the majority of African Americans first learn to read; In the period between 1900 and 1920, millions of African Americans will leave the south to move north in what is known as the Great Migration.

1903—W.E.B. DuBois publishes *The Souls of Black Folks.*

1904—African Americans begin to move in large numbers into Harlem, a neighborhood in New York City, when Philip A. Payton, Jr., an African-American realtor, founds the Afro-American Realty Company.

1906—DuBois and others start the Niagara Movement, which includes African-American thinkers who aim to bring about racial equality in the United States.

1909—A new organization, the National Association for the Advancement of Colored People (NAACP), is founded.

1916—Marcus Garvey moves to the United States.

1919—The year many historians believe the Harlem Renaissance begins; Some say the period's first literary work is Claude McKay's poem, "If We Must Die."

1921—The Harlem branch of the New York Public Library holds an exhibition of art works by African-American artists.

1923—*Opportunity,* an African-American literary and political magazine, first appears.

1924—Poet Langston Hughes moves to Harlem; About the same time, Zora Neale Hurston, the most important female writer of the Harlem Renaissance, arrives.

1925—James Weldon Johnson describes Harlem as a mecca for African Americans; *Survey Magazine* devotes an entire issue to what it calls the "New Negro"; Alain Locke will turn its essays into a book of the same name; Garland Anderson becomes the first African-American playwright to have a play performed on Broadway.

1926—Hughes, Hurston, and others launch a new magazine called *Fire!*; Only one issue appears, but it demonstrates that not all African Americans agree as to what they should be writing.

1929—The year many historians regard as the end of the Harlem Renaissance; In October, the stock market crashes, beginning the Great Depression.

1930s—The people of Harlem, like others all over America, suffer through the Depression; As money becomes a problem, fewer people can earn a living as writers, artists, and photographers; Jazz music, however, continues to flourish.

1969—The Metropolitan Museum of Art mounts an exhibit celebrating the Harlem Renaissance called "Harlem on My Mind."

★ CHAPTER NOTES ★

Chapter 1. Rent Parties

1. Willie "the Lion" Smith and George Hoefer, *Music on My Mind: The Memoirs of an American Pianist* (New York: Doubleday & Company, 1964), pp. 152–153.

2. Langston Hughes, *The Big Sea* (New York: Hill and Wang, 1963), p. 153.

3. Jeff Kisseloff, *You Must Remember This: An Oral History of Manhattan from the 1890s to World War II* (New York: Harcourt Brace Jovanovich, 1989), p. 324.

4. Frank Byrd, "Rent Parties," *A Renaissance in Harlem: Lost Voices of an American Community*, ed. Lionel C. Bascom (New York: Avon Books, 1999), p. 64.

5. Ernest J. Wilson, "Mae's Rent Party," in *Poetry of the Negro, 1946–1970* and Wallace Thurman, *The Blacker the Berry* (New York: Arno Press and the New York Times, 1969), pp. 157–213.

6. Hughes, pp. 228–229, 233.

7. Vicki Howard, "The Joint is Jumpin': Harlem Rent Parties in the 1920s," n.d., <http://www.dla.utexas.edu/depts/ams/Jazz/Jazz2/Howard.html> (June 28, 2000).

8. Arnold Rampersad, "Introduction," *The New Negro*, ed. Alain Locke (New York: Atheneum, 1992), p. ix.

Chapter 2. African Americans After the Civil War

1. Daniel M. Johnson and Rex R. Campbell, *Black Migration in America* (Durham: Duke University Press, 1981), p. 49.

2. Booker T. Washington, *Up from Slavery* (New York: Dodd, Mead, 1965), p. 29.

3. Ibid., pp. 38–39.

4. Booker T. Washington, "Freedom," *Eyewitness to America: 500 Years of America in the Words of Those Who Saw It Happen*, ed. David Colbert (New York: Pantheon Books, 1997), p. 248.

5. John Hope Franklin, *From Slavery to Freedom: A History of Negro Americans* (New York: Alfred A. Knopf, 1980), pp. 262–264.

6. Andrew Carroll, ed., *Letters of a Nation* (New York: Kodansha International, 1997), p. 190.

7. Lionel Bascom, "Introduction: History from the Ground Up," *A Renaissance in Harlem: Lost Voices of an American Community*, ed. Lionel C. Bascom (New York: Avon Books, 1999), p. 5.

8. W.E.B. DuBois, "I. Of Our Spiritual Strivings," *Selection from W.E.B DuBois' The Souls of Black Folks Part 1, 1903 (1901)*, n.d., <http://www.albany.edu/faculty/gz580/his101/webdub2.html> (October 29, 2001).

9. David L. Lewis, *W.E.B. DuBois* (New York: Holt, 1993), p. 293.

10. "Harlem Renaissance," n.d., <http://www.pbs.org/newshour/forum/february98/harlem_2-20.html> (June 18, 2000).

11. Lewis, p. 291.

12. Manning Marable, *W.E.B. Dubois: Black Radical Democrat* (Boston: Twayne Publishers, 1986), p. 73.

13. African American Studies Program at the University of Puget Sound, "The Crisis," *Documents in African American History*, n.d., <http://www.ups.edu/history/afamhis/documents/crisis.htm> (January 2001).

14. Lewis, p. 324.

15. Fred Howard, *Wilbur and Orville: A Biography of the Wright Brothers* (Norwalk, Conn.: Eastern Press, 1987), p. 8.

16. Robert E. Spiller et al., eds., *Literary History of the United States: History* (New York: MacMillan, 1974), p. 748.

17. Paul Lawrence Dunbar, "The Colored Soldiers," *Majors and Minors*, 1895, <http://www.libraries.wright.edu/dunbar/majors1.html#majors10> (October 29, 2001).

Chapter 3. Harlem, New York, and the Great Migration

1. Daniel M. Johnson and Rex R. Campbell, *Black Migration in America* (Durham: Duke University Press, 1981), pp. 71–72.

2. Cary D. Wintz, *Black Culture and the Harlem Renaissance* (Houston: Rice University Press, 1988), pp. 20–21.

3. "A Brief History of Harlem," n.d., <http://www.harlemontime.com/tour/main.html> (June 29, 2000).

4. James Weldon Johnson, "Harlem: The Culture Capital," *The New Negro*, ed. Alain Locke (New York: A. and C. Boni, 1925), p. 302.

5. Wintz, pp. 18–20.

6. Henry Rhodes, "The Social Contributions of the Harlem Renaissance," *Yale-New Haven Teachers Institute*, n.d., <http://www.yale.edu/ynhti/curriculum/units/1978/2/78.02.08.x.html> (October 29, 2001).

7. James Weldon Johnson, p. 309.

8. Ibid., p. 301.

9. Arnold Rampersad, "Introduction," *The New Negro*, ed. Alain Locke (New York: Atheneum, 1992), p. x.

10. James Weldon Johnson, p. 301.

11. James Weldon Johnson, *Black Manhattan*, in Caroline Jackson, "Harlem Renaissance: Pivotal Period in the Development of Afro-American Culture," *Yale-New Haven Teachers Institute*, 1998, <http://www.yale.edu/ynhti/curriculum/units/1978/2/78.02.03.x.html> (July 1, 2000).

Chapter 4. The Renaissance Begins

1. Lionel C. Bascom, "Introduction: History from the Ground Up," *A Renaissance in Harlem: Lost Voices of an American Community*, ed. Lionel C. Bascom (New York: Avon Books, 1999), p. 2.

2. "Marcus Garvey and UNIA Papers Project," 1995, <http://www.isop.ucla.edu/mgpp/sample01.htm> (March 19, 2001).

3. Carole Marks and Diana Edkins, *The Power of Pride* (New York: Crown Publishers, Inc., 1999), pp. 80–81.

4. Curtis Skinner, "Johnson, James Weldon 1871–1938," in Hal May and Susan M. Trotsky, eds., *Contemporary Authors* (Detroit: Gale Research, Inc., 1989), vol. 125, p. 237.

5. James Weldon Johnson, "Lift Every Voice and Sing," *James Weldon Johnson (1871–1938)*, n.d., <http://www.nku.edu/~diesmanj/johnson.html#lifteveryvoice> (January 12, 2001).

6. Marks and Edkins, p. 82.

7. Ibid., p. 86.

8. "The Creation, James Weldon Johnson," *The Academy of American Poets*, n.d., <http://www.poets.org/poems/Poemprnt.cfm?prmID=1443> (March 19, 2001).

9. James Weldon Johnson, *God's Trombones* (New York: Penguin Books, 1990), pp. 14–15.

10. Henry Rhodes, "The Social Contributions of the Harlem Renaissance," n.d., <http://www.yale.edu/ynhti/curriculum/units/1978/2/78.02.08.x.html> (October 29, 2001).

11. From *The Collected Poems of Langston Hughes* by Langston Hughes, © 1994 by The Estate of Langston Hughes. Used by permission of Alfred A. Knopf, a division of Random House, Inc.

12. Ibid.

13. Ibid.

14. Arnold Rampersad, "Introduction," *The New Negro,* ed. Alain Locke (New York: Atheneum, 1992), pp. x–xi.

15. Levi Hubert, "Whites Invade Harlem," *A Renaissance in Harlem: Lost Voices of an American Community*, ed. Lionel C. Bascom (New York: Avon Books, 1999), p. 24.

16. Alain Locke, "Enter the New Negro," n.d., <http://etext.lib.virginia.edu/harlem/LocEnteF.html> (October 29, 2001).

17. Laurie Dickinson, "Zora Neale Hurston (1891–1960)," *Voices From the Gaps: Women Writers of Color*, n.d., <http://voices.cla.umn.edu/authors/ZoraNealeHurston.html> (October 29, 2001).

18. "Chronology," *Zora Neale Hurston,* n.d., <http://www.geocities.com/kiphinton/zora/zchronol.htm> (October 29, 2001).

19. Zora Neale Hurston, "Spunk," *Poetry and Prose of the Harlem Renaissance,* n.d., <http://www.nku.edu/~diesmanj/spunk.html> (March 19, 2001).

20. Hubert, p. 26.

21. Cary D. Wintz, *Black Culture and the Harlem Renaissance* (Houston: Rice University Press, 1988), p. 85.

22. Hubert, p. 26.

23. Ibid., p. 27.

Chapter 5. Music and the Theater

1. James Weldon Johnson, "Negro Songmakers (1930)," in Lindsay Patterson, ed., *The Negro in Music and Art Volume from the International Library of Negro Life and History* (New York: The Association for the Study of Negro Life and History, 1969), p. 46.

2. "About Harry Lawrence Freeman," *Harry Lawrence Freeman*, March 16, 2000, <http://www.hapka.com/usopera/composers/freeman/> (October 29, 2001).

3. *Creative Fire* (Alexandria, Va.: Time Life Books, 1993), p. 72.

4. Edward A. Berlin, "A Biography of Scott Joplin," *Scott Joplin International Ragtime Foundation*, 1998, <http://www.scottjoplin.org/bios.html> (October 29, 2001).

5. Arnold Rampersad, "Introduction," *The New Negro*, ed. Alain Locke (New York: Atheneum, 1992), p. x.

6. "Fletcher Henderson," *Jazz, A film by Ken Burns*, n.d., <http://www.pbs.org/jazz/biography/artist_id_henderson_fletcher.htm> (December 20, 2001).

7. Samuel A. Floyd, "Music in the Harlem Renaissance: An Overview," *Black Music in the Harlem Renaissance*, ed. Samuel A. Floyd (Westport, Conn.: Greenwood Press, 1990), p. 21.

8. Mark Tucker, "Duke Ellington," *Black Music in the Harlem Renaissance*, ed. Samuel A. Floyd (Westport, Conn.: Greenwood Press, 1990), p. 112.

9. Paul P. Reuben, "Chapter 9: Harlem Renaissance—A Brief Introduction," *PAL: Perspectives in American Literature: A Research and Reference Guide*, February 25, 2001, <http://www.csustan.edu/english/reuben/pal/chap9/9intro.html> (October 29, 2001).

10. "Lilly Lido," *Library of Congress: American Memory*, n.d., <http://loc.gov> (March 19, 2001).

11. Jeffrey P. Green, "The Negro Renaissance and England," *Black Music in the Harlem Renaissance*, ed. Samuel A. Floyd (Westport, Conn.: Greenwood Press, 1990), p. 159.

12. James V. Hatch and Ted Shine, eds., *Black Theatre USA* (New York: The Free Press, 1996), p. 131.

13. Ibid, p. 134.

14. Ibid, p. 168.

15. Ibid., pp. 216–217.

16. James V. Hatch and Leo Hamalian, eds., *Lost Plays of the Harlem Renaissance, 1920–1940* (Detroit: Wayne State University Press, 1996), p. 449.

17. Ibid., pp. 451–452.

Chapter 6. Art

1. *Harlem Renaissance Art of Black America* (New York: Harry N. Abrams, Inc., 1987), p. 110.

2. The Schomburg Center for Research in Black Culture. "Aaron Douglas (1898–1979)," *Exhibition*, n.d., <http://www.si.umich.edu/CHICO/Harlem/text/adouglas.html> (December 4, 2001).

3. "Palmer Hayden," n.d., <http://www.donegal.k12.pa.us/dms/Kif/palmer.htm> (January 12, 2001).

4. *Harlem Renaissance Art of Black America*, pp. 179–181.

5. Reginald McGhee, *The World of James Van Derzee: A Visual Record of Black Americans* (New York: Grove Press, 1969), pp. 5–6.

6. *Creative Fire* (Alexandria, Va.: Time Life Books, 1993), p. 213.

Chapter 7. The End of the Harlem Renaissance

1. Elliott V. Bell, "The Wall Street Crash, New York," The *Mammoth Book of Eye-witness History*, ed. Jon E. Lewis (New York: Carroll & Graf Publishers, Inc., 1998), p. 371.

2. Paul S. Boyer et al., *The Enduring Vision: A History of the American People*, second edition (Lexington, Mass.: D.C. Health and Company, 1993), p. 839.

3. Ibid., p. 873.

4. Frank Byrd, "Afternoon in a Pushcart Peddlers' Colony," *A Renaissance in Harlem: Lost Voices of an American Community*, ed. Lionel C. Bascom (New York: Avon Books, 1999), pp. 85, 90; Frank Byrd and Terry Roth, "Street Cries and Criers," *A Renaissance in Harlem: Lost Voices of an American Community*, ed. Lionel C. Bascom (New York: Avon Books, 1999), p. 90.

5. Lionel C. Bascom, "Visible Men," *A Renaissance in Harlem: Lost Voices of an American Community*, ed. Lionel C. Bascom (New York: Avon Books, 1999), p. 34.

6. Mark Helbling, *The Harlem Renaissance: The One and the Many* (Westport, Conn.: Greenwood Press, 1999), p. 1.

7. Bascom, p. 84.

8. *A Brief History of Harlem*, 1995–1998, <http://www.harlem-ontime.com/tour/main.html> (October 30, 2001).

9. David N. Dinkins, "Foreword," *A Brief History of Harlem*, 1995–1998, <http://www.harlem-ontime.com/tour/main.html> (October 30, 2001).

10. "New York City: Historical Context," *Soul of America*, n.d., <http://www.soulofamerica.com/cityfldr/nyc1.html> (October 30, 2001).

Chapter 8. The Legacy of the Harlem Renaissance

1. Lionel C. Bascom, "Minstrel Show," *A Renaissance in Harlem: Lost Voices of an American Community*, ed. Lionel C. Bascom (New York: Avon Books, 1999), p. 23.

2. "Harlem Renaissance," *Online News Hour Forum*, February 20, 1998, <http://www.pbs.org/newshour.forum/february98/harlem_2-20.html> (June 18, 2000).

3. Levi Hubert, "Whites Invade Harlem," *A Renaissance in Harlem: Lost Voices of an American Community*, ed. Lionel C. Bascom (New York: Avon Books, 1999), p. 24.

4. "Session Twenty-Five," *The Harlem Renaissance*, n.d., <http://humanities.byu.edu/classes/hum262ab/session25.htm> (October 30, 2001).

★ FURTHER READING ★

Books

Chambers, Veronica. *Harlem Renaissance.* Philadelphia: Chelsea House Publishers, 1997.

Feinstein, Stephen. *The 1920s From Prohibition to Charles Lindbergh.* Berkeley Heights, N.J.: Enslow Publishers, Inc., 2001.

Haskins, James. *The Harlem Renaissance.* Brookfield, Conn.: Millbrook Press, Inc., 1996.

Internet Addresses

The Academy of American Poets. "Poets of the Harlem Renaissance and After." *Poetry Exhibits.* 1997–2000. <http://www.poets.org/exh/Exhibit.cfm?prmID=7>.

Dinkins, David N. "Foreword." *A Brief History of Harlem.* 1995–1998. <http://www.harlem-ontime.com/tour/main.html>.

Reuben, Paul P. "Chapter 9: Harlem Renaissance–A Brief Introduction." *PAL: Perspectives in American Literature: A Research and Reference Guide.* February 25, 2001. <http://www.csustan.edu/english/reuben/pal/chap9/9intro.html>.

★ INDEX ★

A

African Americans
    and the Depression, 87–88
    education, 16–23
    following the Civil War,
        13–16
    and Harlem, 7, 11–12, 30,
        32, 35, 37–39, 94, 96
    and the Harlem
        Renaissance, 11, 55–56,
        64, 72, 90, 91, 94–95
    migration, 7, 13, 31–33,
        35, 55
    and voting rights, 15, 16
Anderson, Garland, 75
Armstrong, Louis, 69, 90

B

blues music, 64, 67

C

Chesnutt, Charles Waddell,
    26–27
classical music, 63–64, 71
The Crisis, 25, 80

D

Depression, 86–88
Douglas, Aaron, 78–80
DuBois, W.E.B., 21–26, 67
Dunbar, Paul Laurence,
    27–30, 31

E

Ellington, Duke, 69–71
Ellison, Ralph, 90–91

G

Garvey, Marcus, 41–44, 85
Great Migration, 31–33, 35,
    55

Grimké, Angelina Weld, 73

H

Hampton Institute, 16–17
Harlem, 99
    and African Americans, 7,
        11–12, 30, 32, 35,
        37–39, 94, 96
    and the Depression, 88–89
    following the Harlem
        Renaissance, 93
    history, 35–37
Harlem Renaissance, 93
    and African Americans, 11,
        55–56, 64, 72, 90, 91,
        94–95
    and the arts, 11–12, 49,
        57, 61–62, 64, 72, 74,
        78, 85, 90, 91, 96
    beginning, 49
    definition, 11
    and the Depression, 88, 90
    legacy, 97, 99
    and rent parties, 11
Hayden, Palmer, 82–83
Hughes, Langston, 49–52,
    58–59, 76, 90, 95
Hurston, Zora Neale, 56–59,
    76, 90

J

jazz music, 10, 66–67, 69–71
Johnson, James Weldon, 38,
    44–48

K

Ku Klux Klan (KKK), 15

L

Locke, Alain, 54–56, 58–59,
    67, 79, 94

M
McKay, Claude, 48–49
musicals, 71–72

N
National Association for the
    Advancement of Colored
    People (NAACP), 25, 39,
    46, 88
"New Negro," 55, 56
The New Negro, 54–56,
    58–59, 71, 79
Niagara Movement, 24–26

O
opera music, 62, 63
*Opportunity: A Journal of
    Negro Life*, 52–54, 80

P
Prohibition, 9–10

R
ragtime music, 64, 66
rent parties, 8–11
Richardson, Willis, 74–75

S
Savage, Augusta, 77–78

segregation, 14–15, 69
sharecropping, 13–14, 19,
    87–88
The Souls of Black Folks,
    23–24

T
Talented Tenth, 22–23
theater, 72–76
Tuskegee Institute, 18–20

U
Universal Negro
    Improvement Association
    (UNIA), 42–44, 85
Urban League, 39, 52, 88

V
Van Der Zee, James, 83–84, 90

W
Washington, Booker
    Taliaferro, 16–21, 22, 25
Works Progress
    Administration (WPA)
    Writer's Project, 89–90
World War I, 40